THE NEXT ECONOMY MBA

Redesigning Business for
the Benefit of All Life

THE NEXT ECONOMY MBA

LIFT ECONOMY in Association with
**ERIN AXELROD, KEVIN BAYUK, SHAWN BERRY,
RYAN HONEYMAN,** and **PHOENIX SOLEIL**

Berrett–Koehler Publishers, Inc.

Berrett-Koehler Publishers, Inc.
1333 Broadway, Suite 1000
Oakland, CA 94612-1921
Tel: (510) 817-2277
Fax: (510) 817-2278
www.bkconnection.com

ORDERING INFORMATION

Quantity sales. Special discounts are available on quantity purchases by corporations, associations, and others. For details, contact the "Special Sales Department" at the Berrett-Koehler address above.

Individual sales. Berrett-Koehler publications are available through most bookstores. They can also be ordered directly from Berrett-Koehler: Tel: (800) 929-2929; Fax: (802) 864-7626; www.bkconnection.com.

Orders for college textbook / course adoption use. Please contact Berrett-Koehler: Tel: (800) 929-2929; Fax: (802) 864-7626.

Distributed to the U.S. trade and internationally by Penguin Random House Publisher Services.

Berrett-Koehler and the BK logo are registered trademarks of Berrett-Koehler Publishers, Inc.

Printed in Canada

Berrett-Koehler books are printed on long-lasting acid-free paper. When it is available, we choose paper that has been manufactured by environmentally responsible processes. These may include using trees grown in sustainable forests, incorporating recycled paper, minimizing chlorine in bleaching, or recycling the energy produced at the paper mill.

Library of Congress Cataloging-in-Publication Data

Names: LIFT Economy (San Francisco, California), author. | Axelrod, Erin, author.
Title: The next economy MBA : redesigning business for the benefit of all life / LIFT Economy in Association with Erin Axelrod, Kevin Bayuk, Shawn Berry, Ryan Honeyman, and Phoenix Soleil.
Description: First Edition. | Oakland, CA : Berrett-Koehler Publishers, [2023] | Includes bibliographical references and index.
    Identifiers: LCCN 2022051591 (print) | LCCN 2022051592 (ebook) | ISBN 9781523002573 (paperback) | ISBN 9781523002580 (pdf) | ISBN 9781523002597 (epub) | ISBN 9781523002603 (audio)
Subjects: LCSH: Master of business administration degree. | Business Education—History—21st century. | Organizational change—History—21st century. | Consumption (Economics) | Climatic changes—Economic aspects. | Climatic changes—Social aspects.
Classification: LCC HF1111 .L54 2023 (print) | LCC HF1111 (ebook) | DDC 650.071/173—dc23/eng/20230126
LC record available at https://lccn.loc.gov/2022051591
LC ebook record available at https://lccn.loc.gov/2022051592

First Edition
30 29 28 27 26 25 24 23   10 9 8 7 6 5 4 3 2 1

Cover Design: Adam Johnson
Interior design and composition: Seventeenth Street Studios

CONTENTS

FOREWORD

I met the LIFT Economy team in 2018, shortly after the release of the first edition of my book, *Decolonizing Wealth: Indigenous Wisdom to Heal Divides and Restore Balance* (Berrett-Koehler). Joining them on their *Next Economy Now* podcast allowed me to connect to a similar-minded organization working to heal and reimagine our economy. I immediately knew that LIFT Economy would be a coconspirator in our collective work to decolonize wealth by providing tools, resources, and support to entrepreneurs who endeavor to shift the economy towards our shared values of racial justice, repair, joy, healing, and collective liberation.

I often present a critical analysis of how money has been accumulated and how it flows through markets and communities. Even in the realms of philanthropy, social finance, and investment, colonialism is the core ailment prohibiting true equity in the sector. The "colonizer virus," as I coined it, continues to divide, control, and extract from our cultures and ways of being, hindering the ability of Black, Indigenous, and other communities of color and marginalized populations to thrive. Our current economic system intentionally prevents the economic prosperity of those it subjugates. And even well-intentioned leaders who manage and control the flow of money reinforce the colonial divisions of the "us vs. them" paradigm. For example, older white men are usually in charge of giving (and hoarding) money, while people of color are often pitted against each other to compete for resources that those in power make falsely scarce. These colonial dynamics continue to hold true in the global economy—and will into the future, until we commit to healing. We must imagine a different way of using money.

Instead of a tool used to divide, separate, control, and exploit, can money foster connection, belonging, and healing? I often ask, how can we use money as medicine? How can we use money for the sacred purpose of restoring balance, of healing our communities, our families, businesses, and cities?

The Next Economy MBA offers some critical answers for entrepreneurs. This book invites us first to examine the roots of many inequitable systems and structures. It provides key building blocks for a new kind of business education—one that is needed to create a racially just, environmentally regenerative, and locally self-reliant economy that works for the benefit of all life. For individuals aspiring to be part of this new way, it is no small feat to create a business that is aligned with this vision. *The Next Economy MBA* is a guide for the journey—delivering a clear picture of what is possible and equipping us with practical tools and techniques needed to achieve the human-centered vision we have for our businesses.

Decolonizing—or healing—our minds, hearts, and spirits is how we will be able to reimagine an economy that centers people and the planet. This is how we create a world where our systems and ways of being support racial equity—so everyone can live their best lives, thrive in their cultures, and bring about healing from generations of colonial trauma. *The Next Economy MBA* is a generous resource for those on the journey of reimagining and actualizing this vision. It's on all of us to redesign the economy so that it benefits all life. This book helps show you how your work can be a part of it.

—Edgar Villanueva, author, activist, philanthropist;
founder/principal, Decolonizing Wealth Project and Liberated Capital

INTRODUCTION

I want to be a doula to the Next Economy. It will take many of us to bring on the birth, but it is time. Time to rematriate our world, our Mother Earth.

The Next Economy needs to be restorative and regenerative. It needs to not poison people and land. No more "-cides" in the food and in the water. That stuff will kill you. It needs to be compassionate and maternal—looking out for relatives, whether they have hands, paws, roots, claws, or fins.

The Next Economy has efficiency, organic food, electric trains, restorative justice, renewable energy, and quality support for women and children. That's the economy I want.

—Winona LaDuke, "Doula to the Next Economy"[1]

Welcome. Thank you for being here. If you are reading this book, you are probably like us ("us," "we," and "our" refer to the authors of this book), dismayed about things like the racial wealth divide, the climate crisis, the wielding of finance as a tool of oppression, and other deep systemic imbalances. How did society get to, in the words of Movement Generation, a world of "banks and tanks" instead of "caring and cooperation"?[2] And how does humanity move closer to a world where everyone's needs are met?

The Business as Usual Economy

It is clear that the current system, which we refer to as the "Business as Usual" (or BAU) economy, is not working for the vast majority of people and the planet. For us, calling it "Business as Usual" is used to confer a sense of possibility for change and as an omen of the risk of complacency (we try to avoid using "capitalism" because, as with "socialism" or "communism," there are often strong feelings associated with the term). For example, as a result of the BAU economy:

- A tiny group of white men have more wealth than billions of people.[3]
- About 800 million people go hungry or malnourished each day, even though twice the number of calories needed to feed all of humanity are produced.[4]
- Two billion people still lack safely managed drinking water.[5]
- One million species of plants and animals are at risk of extinction, and the extinction list grows monthly.[6]
- Greenhouse gas emissions from agriculture, land exploitation, and fossil fuel combustion have radically altered the atmosphere of the planet, creating an existential risk to human life in the form of climate chaos from global warming.[7]
- White supremacy and extremism are on the rise globally.[8]
- The racial wealth "gap" is not merely a gap, but an enormous chasm that continues to grow at an alarming rate.[9]

All of these crises can be connected back to the core systems, structures, and norms of the BAU economy. In order for humanity to have a livable future, the BAU economy must die out—or at least be radically transformed.

The Next Economy

The "Next Economy" is our name for an economic system that works for people and the planet. We imagine the Next Economy as a bioregional, locally self-reliant, and racially just economy that works for the benefit of all life—one that meets basic needs for all people everywhere while regenerating planetary ecosystems. The Next Economy is both an aspirational vision and something that partially exists today. The transformation of the economic system to one that benefits all life could take hundreds of years. However, we believe there can be significant progress towards that goal in a much shorter time frame. Indeed, we joyfully acknowledge that there are whispers, songs, dances, and actions that highlight the radical transformation already underway all around us.

Some readers may wonder why we use the term "Next Economy" instead of "New Economy." This is because many of the systems, approaches, and solutions that we will see in the Next Economy are actually quite old (e.g., Indigenous wisdom, gift economy, locally self-reliant practices).

What Is This Book About?

The central question this book is trying to answer is "What would a business education look like if the goal were to redesign the economy for the benefit of all life?" The *Next Economy MBA* is for people who want to strengthen their understanding of business fundamentals for stewarding an organization (vision, culture, strategy, operations, etc.) from a racially just and environmentally regenerative perspective. This book will detail the growing number of structures, principles, and practices that are helping to create more equitable and beneficial out-comes for all.

We are writing this book—and since 2017 have been facilitating an online course called the Next Economy MBA—because many people are seeking an affordable and easily accessible education in regen-erative business. Most current MBA programs do not meet this need. Prospective MBA students want to explore possibilities and pathways that help shift the needle towards transformational change.

At the same time, we want to acknowledge that not every concept in this book is radical and revolutionary. Many ideas in this book—visioning, goal setting, recruiting, compensation, strategic positioning, creating a core value proposition, creating operating projections, and more—have their foundation in "business 101" and common BAU practices.

We also want to be clear that we do not believe that all BAU prac-tices are necessarily bad. Certain widespread business practices can be useful in helping to build the Next Economy. For example, "rapid pro-totyping," used by many traditional businesses, is a process in which you create a rough draft of a potential product or service offering, get that idea in front of potential customers, collect feedback, and quickly refine and iterate your idea based on that feedback. The widespread use of rapid prototyping (also referred to as "build, measure, and learn" cycles) does not mean Next Economy organizations should avoid using this approach for their own product or service design. Quite the contrary—we believe many Next Economy organizations could benefit from using build, measure, and learn cycles. The transition to a better future requires radical and transformative practices—and it requires tweaking, revising, and shifting traditional BAU practices to better align them with Next Economy principles.

Why Is LIFT Economy Writing This Book?

We are writing this book, and are passionate about redesigning the economy, for two main reasons. First, it is ecocidal and suicidal to not transform the BAU economy. We want a livable future for our families, for our communities, and for all of life. Second, we see the latent potential all around us. Humanity has not scratched the surface of the abundance, joy, connection, peace, and reliable prosperity that is possible for all beings. This is why we have committed our life energy to furthering this transformation to the Next Economy.

We are basing the content in this book on our work with more than 300 social enterprises over the past decade. This includes our work with smaller, more radical companies such as Winona's Hemp & Heritage Farm, the East Bay Permanent Real Estate Cooperative, the Tribal EcoRestoration Alliance, Our Table Cooperative, and GreenWave. It also includes our work with larger social enterprises such as Patagonia, Ben & Jerry's, Allbirds, Madewell, and Thrive Market. The content in this book has also been influenced by the 500-plus alumni of multiple cohorts of the Next Economy MBA online course who provided us with feedback about how to make it better.

The Structure of This Book

The order of topics in this book is not random and is similar to the presentation of the Next Economy MBA online course. It has been carefully designed to lead you along a path, with major stops corresponding to the nine parts summarized below.

- **Part 1: Intro to the Next Economy.** The start of this journey together is defining a shared language and understanding. Creating the Next Economy is not possible without agreement on shared language. For example, what does the word *economy* mean, how is it being used, and why is your understanding of that word important? Another opportunity is cocreating a more detailed picture of your end goal. What would the Next Economy look like? How would you know you have achieved it? This vision stands in stark contrast to the existing BAU economy. There are many reasons why the BAU economy is not working. It is clear that it needs to change. What are the transition frameworks? How does society get from here to there?

- **Part 2: Principles of Next Economy Enterprises.** There is no clearly defined set of steps you need to follow to create the Next Economy. The process is emergent. However, there are Next Economy principles that you can use to guide your efforts to start, grow, and develop organizations (companies, enterprises, nonprofits, etc.) that will deliver needed goods and services to your community in ways that benefit all life. What principles can you use to design and operate your organization to be part of the transitional journey? What evidence is there to illustrate that these principles work?

- **Part 3: Enterprise Structures and Legal Frameworks.** The principles of Next Economy organizations are not enough by themselves. The BAU economy has operating structures and legal systems that favor the status quo and suppress change. Thankfully, people have been working to build new structures and hack old structures in order to change their operating systems. What structures are available? Which ones would allow your organization to best express Next Economy principles?

- **Part 4: Personal Strategies and Life Design.** An economy that works for the benefit of all life is not possible without also changing yourself. What are the consumption patterns, habits, behaviors, and norms you need to change? What is your purpose for being alive? What unique contribution can you make to the movement? How do you design your life to better align with your vision for the Next Economy?

- **Part 5: Vision Alignment.** You have an introduction to the Next Economy. You have learned about the principles of Next Economy organizations. You have learned about legal structures and life design. What if you wanted to start (or grow) an organization and express those principles? What are some keys to success? Where do organizations typically get tripped up and fail? In our experience, the biggest determinant of an organization's success or failure is whether or not they have an aligned vision for the impact they would like to create in the world.

- **Part 6: Culture.** The next priority is culture. If your team has a shared vision, but you lack a set of core values, cannot effectively communicate with each other, and do not have an equitable, inclusive, and democratic culture, your enterprise likely will not work. What are the critical components of building a supportive, collaborative, and inspired culture that can sustain your team through the long journey to your future vision?

- **Part 7: Strategy.** Your strategy allows you to bring your products or services to market. You need to understand how to perform market and industry research, design and position your offering, and communicate your core value proposition. Designing governance processes and raising money from investors or accessing resources from your community should be done thoughtfully. This section also explores finance, the order of operations for seeking finance, available security structure options, and how to find the right investors.

- **Part 8: Operational Systems.** The last component of designing your enterprise involves creating an organizational structure, roles, responsibilities, and tasks; creating an operating projection and financial system; instituting policies and procedures; and improving your personal productivity systems. Getting your vision, culture, strategy, and operational systems functioning and evolving gives your organization a good chance of long-term impact.

- **Part 9: Next Steps for the Next Economy.** You have learned the key components of creating sustained impact as an organization. How do you move beyond one organization? How do you change the whole system? Successful Next Economy organizations need to federate and collaborate to change whole systems such as governance, healthcare, education, media, and housing. The long arc of transition aims to compassionately hospice out the BAU economy and midwife in the Next Economy.

Case Studies, Workbook, Definitions, and Disclaimers

This journey can sometimes feel lonely and daunting. You might be wondering, "Am I the only one trying to do this?" or "Is this really possible?" We have included several case studies, spread throughout the book, that demonstrate that the Next Economy is not only possible, but already exists and is growing. Each case study lists which of the ten principles of Next Economy organizations the focus of the case study embodies. The goal is to give you better insight into different designs of Next Economy organizations. For more details, the ten principles of Next Economy organizations are described in detail in Part 2: Principles of Next Economy Enterprises.

This book may bring up more questions for you. We created *Next Economy MBA: Read-Along Workbook* as a free resource to help you clarify your goals and objectives, practice new skills, and go deeper on your journey. This workbook is a companion to this book—the book has the teachings and the workbook has the exercises. This workbook was developed for individual use or as part of a team or group exercise. You can certainly do this work on your own, but it can be more powerful with other people. Download the workbook for free by visiting lifteconomy.com/mbabook.

Many of the concepts in this book are universal. You will find this book to be relevant regardless of your location and your organizational type (corporation, solopreneur, LLC, nonprofit, philanthropic foundation, etc.). For ease of communication, we use the terms "company," "business," "enterprise," and "organization" somewhat interchangeably throughout the book. Even if you work for a nonprofit or other organizational type, we encourage you to apply or adapt the concepts in this book to your situation.

Please note that the LIFT partners who are co-authoring this book are not credentialed legal professionals. Nothing shared in this book should be construed by you as legal advice. When considering certain actions—particularly when choosing a legal structure and pursuing a financing strategy—we recommend that you speak with an attorney to ensure any actions you take comply with local laws and regulations.

Finally, this book offers a summary overview of our facilitated Next Economy MBA online course. For folks who want to go deeper, we recommend joining one of our live Next Economy MBA cohorts. Many course participants have found that the more in-depth content—combined with learning alongside a supportive, mission-aligned group of emerging leaders—has been transformative. The online courses are offered every spring and fall. Please see lifteconomy.com/mba on the LIFT website for more details about upcoming sessions.

We hope the principles, stories, and entrepreneurs described in this book will empower, equip, and inspire you to join in, in whatever way you can. We need you. We believe in cocreating an economy that works for the benefit of all life together. We hope you will join us.

1

Introduction to the Next Economy

T o start this journey together we need to define a shared language and co-create a more detailed picture of the end goal. For example, what would the Next Economy look like? How would you know you have achieved it? This section also explores the transition frameworks and how society gets from here to there.

What Is the Economy?

When imagining what constitutes "the economy," you might envision things like money, corporations, contracts, the stock market, banks, workers, and international trade. This is not the whole story. The words *economy* and *ecology* share the same etymological root: The prefix *eco-* comes from the Greek word *oikos,* meaning "house," "household," or "family." The suffix *-logy* means "to study" and the suffix *-nomy* means "to manage." Therefore, *ecology* refers to the "study of the house" (or the study of planet Earth) and *economy* refers to the "management of the house."

At LIFT, we define the economy as "a collective set of strategies we use to meet basic human needs." These basic needs include, but are not limited to, nourishing food, clean water, clean air, clothing, shelter, and safety. Focus on meeting needs can unleash a tremendous amount of creativity because it helps clarify the strategies that become available to us. These strategies are often culturally invisible and sometimes referred to as the "informal economy" (e.g., growing surplus food in your backyard and sharing it with neighbors, trading childcare responsibilities with other parents, making or repairing clothing for your household). This reframing of the economy can help you come closer to an understanding of what it could look like to have an economy that works for the benefit of all life.

Vision for an Economy That Works

The Next Economy. The new economy. The regenerative economy. The solidarity economy. The circular economy. They are not all the same thing—but they all point to the idea that people can meet their needs in a way that supports conditions conducive to all life. One exercise we have undertaken over the past few years is to ask participants in our Next Economy MBA online course to imagine what the future might look like if an economy that works for everyone were achieved. In particular, we have asked hundreds of participants "What would the Next Economy look like? What would be different? How would you know you had achieved the goal?" Here is a small sample of some of the answers we have received from folks over the years:

1. **Basic needs:** Everyone has their basic needs met, including access to clothing, shelter, food, water, healthcare, and education.

2. **Regenerative transition:** The dominant extractive economy is not in existence. It has been replaced by a bioregional, equitable, inclusive, communitarian, multi-stakeholder, and locally self-reliant economy that works for the benefit of all life. This has led to a return to preindustrial levels of carbon dioxide. The earth is now growing in biodiversity and abundance.

3. **Equitable leadership, outcomes, and reparation:** There is leadership in all sectors of the economy from Black, Indigenous, and other people of color (BIPOC); women; recent immigrants; people with disabilities; folks who identify as lesbian, gay, bisexual, transgender, queer or questioning, intersex, asexual,

and more (LGBTQIA+); as well as other traditionally marginalized groups. Differences in outcomes of health, wealth, education, housing, and so forth do not correlate with a person belonging to a particular racial or ethnic group. In addition, truth and reconciliation processes have been completed. Full reparations have been given to Black and Indigenous folks.

4. **Indigenous wisdom and sovereignty:** Indigenous wisdom and knowledge is deeply respected and informs all types of decisions. Indigenous teachings are now guiding fire management, flood mitigation, and overall efforts to achieve ecological balance. Native American rights and Indigenous rights around the world have been restored.

5. **Abolition:** Prisons and police have been abolished. Appropriate, timely, and empathetic care is given to all. Transformative justice responds to violence and harm beyond restoration and repair by addressing the systems that produce injustice and oppression.

6. **Liberated children:** Children are physically, emotionally, mentally, and socially free to be curious and inquisitive. Kids are not tucked away while caregivers work. Childcare no longer functions to support the extractive economy's schedule.

7. **Disability justice:** Access is understood as a collective responsibility. Access is centered as a core part of living in the world together. It is seen as a core part of liberation.

8. **Dismantling white supremacy:** All forms of white supremacy have been eradicated. White people are connected to their place-based Indigenous European ancestors, keeping them rooted in culture beyond whiteness.

As you can see, this small list of examples can feel exciting and motivating. Cocreating a more detailed vision of the future will inspire people to move beyond the status quo. This can make it easier to work backwards and identify the steps needed to create a better world.

Psychosocial Critique of the Existing Economy

The BAU economy has deep-seated and systemic problems. Before addressing how to make a transition to the Next Economy, it is important to understand these problems so that it is clear why this transition is needed in the first place. Here are some of the most critical problems:

Problem 1: Interest-Bearing Debt

An increasing percentage of people use money to meet their basic needs. This is problematic because money is most often generated through interest-bearing debt, meaning it is created through the process of being lent out. For example, if you take out a loan, the bank deposits money—which it created out of thin air—into your account and begins charging you interest. One consequence of this is that it generates an artificial need for growth—often via activities that exploit people and the planet—in order to generate enough money to repay the debt and interest. This burden of continual growth has placed extreme pressure on society and the environment. Many people feel forced to participate in this system because they do not have access to alternative strategies that can meet their needs at a lower cost to their mental, emotional, physical, and spiritual health. It is also problematic because it depersonalizes interactions—the opposite of how human needs have historically been met through gifts, bartering, and sharing. You end up with impersonal transactions rather than relationships. You get business instead of community.

Problem 2: A Scarcity Mindset

In Oakland, California, houselessness is a huge challenge ("houseless" and "unhoused" are sometimes used in place of the word "homeless," because many unhoused people feel that they do have homes). Tents and other makeshift structures can be seen under highway overpasses, in industrial areas, and on downtown city streets. In 2022, there were 5,055 houseless people—a 24 percent increase over the previous three years.[10] However, the most recent U.S. census data for the area showed that more than 15,500 housing units remain vacant in Oakland.[11] This shows that there are three times as many vacant houses as houseless people. Similarly, as was mentioned in the Introduction, about 800 million people go hungry or malnourished each day, even though twice the number of calories to feed all of humanity is produced. Scarcity is a fundamental concept of the BAU economy. Often, as in the case of housing and food, resources may be generally plentiful, but distributed in a way that generates scarcity among certain segments of the population.

Problem 3: The Fallacy of the Meritocratic Society

Meritocracy is a political system in which economic benefits and political power are vested in individual people based on talent, effort, and achievement, rather than wealth or social class. We want to call out (in order to hopefully disrupt) that meritocracy is a narrative that has been explicitly championed around the globe to distract from the recognition that colonialism, white supremacy, capitalism, and patriarchy are some of the reasons why inequities exist. It is much easier to keep the power structures in play when folks are directing their attention at individual performance, as opposed to changing the oppressive systems that sustain inequality.

Problem 4: The Fallacy of Progress

The fallacy of progress occurs when generalized economic statistics are put forward as proof that humanity is trending toward growth of well-being and prosperity. Using a single economic measurement like gross domestic product (GDP) to quantify progress for all humanity does not tell the whole story. In this book, and in our live training, we do not use GDP as the measure of progress. For example, in an oil spill, wellbeing and environmental health go down (people who fish out of work, ecosystem collapse, etc.) while GDP may actually increase (through the transactions and expense of clean-up efforts, increased extraction elsewhere, even relief spending). This makes GDP a questionable measurement of "progress." We prefer to reference measures of health and wellbeing, such as the genuine progress indicator (GPI). GPI shows that on a global level, factoring in negative impacts that are not quantified by GDP (including species die-off, overwhelming toxics load, and institutionally enforced incarceration), wellbeing has declined over the past several decades.[12]

Problem 5: ...and Beyond

There are so many more problems. Property ownership, intellectual property silos, the pressure to maximize earnings for shareholders, extractive investment culture, short-term thinking, structural racism, structural sexism, and the externalization of social and environmental harm all need to be addressed. The challenges society faces expand beyond the boundaries of what is traditionally thought of as economy to include the education system, the media system, how humans collectively make sense of information, how to make decisions together, what is valued, and how people live.

Getting from Here to There: Transition Frameworks

Now that we have established a shared language, a vision for the Next Economy, and an analysis and critique of the BAU economy, it can be helpful to offer some frameworks to support humanity's journey from the problems and challenges of the current economy and systems to the Next Economy. The journey can appear long or impossible. It can be difficult to discern what actions to take and which strategies matter. A natural and understandable response to the harms of the BAU economy is to recoil from the pain and grief, to freeze and deny that change is needed, and to filter out information that urgently suggests otherwise.

We have found the Two Loops model developed by the Berkana Institute very useful for making sense of the variety of approaches and paths on the journey to transforming the economic system (indeed, the image on the cover of this book is inspired by that work). The Two Loops model can also help you better understand what role you might play to support the transformation. While we are inspired by the Berkana

Institute's work and want to ensure that all credit for the creation of this model is given to them, for the purposes of our work we emphasize different aspects and interpretations of the Two Loops idea. We encourage you to learn more about how the Berkana Institute uses the model on their website at berkana.org.

The Two Loops model is useful for helping understand the transition from a dominant, old system (BAU economy) to an emergent one (Next Economy) and how to partner with the natural force of evolution to transition to the new and more adaptive system. The model itself is a simple drawing of two curves or loops (Figure 1). The "hospice" curve descends, representing the gradual "death" (or deep transformation or composting) of the existing system (in our case, the BAU economy). The "midwife" curve starts under the hospice curve and moves up, representing the birth or emergence of a new system. Together they represent the journey from now to the full realization of the Next Economy. What does it mean to do hospice and/or midwifery work to transition the economy?

- **Hospice:** Some people, when they become aware of the harms and injustices of the BAU economy, begin to work within (or adjacent to) the existing system, structures, and norms to reduce the harm of the BAU economy, taking incremental actions. Examples include activists pressuring Walmart to commit to 100 percent renewable energy by 2035, or getting Unilever to agree

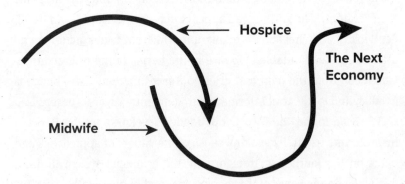

FIGURE 1. The Two Loops Next Economy Transition Model
Source: Lift Economy, adapted from the original Two Loops model developed by the Berkana Institute

to reduce the amount of waste from its products that end up in the landfill, or the years-long effort that has gone into getting investment firms like Goldman Sachs to launch environmental, social, and governance (ESG) public equity investment funds, or campaigns to get Adidas to replace virgin polyester with recycled polyester in products. These hospice actions and strategies are necessary—but wholly inadequate—to effectuate the transition to the Next Economy. People involved in hospicing out the BAU economy can sometimes regard midwife efforts with cynicism. They might refer to midwife efforts as "impractical" because they do not immediately address the perceived problems "at scale." Hospice work is often easier to take on at first because there are more resources and opportunities for personal security available. However, hospice efforts can start to generate cognitive dissonance as it becomes clear that hospice is inadequate to effect the full transformation.

- **Midwife:** Others are not interested in incremental change. They want radical change to the existing systems, structures, and norms. These folks set off to midwife into existence entirely new (or novel, but informed by old-wisdom traditions) forms of organizations, efforts, and lifeways to model what the system might look like after it has already fully transformed. They are inspirational, but midwife strategies come with their own set of challenges. Midwife efforts are often fraught, under-resourced, bereft of personal security, and culturally invisible to society at large. People involved in midwife work often regard hospice work as inadequate and a distraction from the courageous pathfinding work needed to truly transform the economy. Midwife workers may have few opportunities for income and feel extreme pressure to stop the harm of the BAU economy, so sometimes folks involved in more radical work feel antipathy towards anyone not fully engaged in dismantling the existing system as quickly as possible.

It is important to note that this is not a strict binary. Projects can, and often do, have both hospice and midwife elements. In addition, neither hospice work nor midwife work is "better" or "more important" or "more impactful." People need to push firms like Adidas to reduce their environmental footprint as quickly as possible. Simultaneously, new enterprises like Soul Fire Farm—an Afro-Indigenous-centered community farm committed to uprooting racism and seeding sovereignty in the food system—need to be created to model what the Next Economy might look like.

The key insight of the Two Loops model is that both hospice and midwife work is needed. We understand, and empathize with, any resistance you may have to the idea that hospice work and midwife work are equally important. We still grapple with this tension on the LIFT team. Like many of us, you may have developed a strong identity and attachment to the story that there is a clear binary and your type of work is better than the other side. It can feel good, and can reinforce your sense of self, to believe you are on the correct side of the problem. However, binary "us vs. them" thinking is part of the cultural conditioning. It is easier to judge and blame others than to expand the definition of "us." Creating a larger "us" takes vulnerability, courage, humility, and the willingness to listen.

One important insight to help you on this journey is to see hospice and midwife efforts as complementary rather than separate. For example, hospice efforts can sometimes access funding and resources for midwife efforts. Hospice efforts can bring visibility to emergent, Next Economy projects. Midwife efforts can sometimes inspire organizations that were only interested in incremental change to make radical shifts. The Next Economy will be achieved more quickly if you can grow an appreciation for both approaches. Try to identify areas in which hospice and midwife efforts can be mutually supportive and beneficial.

In the next section, we'll examine a set of principles for designing and operating Next Economy organizations. These principles can help you navigate towards a deeper hospicing of the BAU economy and to midwife in novel forms of transformative efforts and behaviors.

2

Principles of Next Economy Enterprises

There is no clearly defined set of steps you need to
follow to create the Next Economy. The process is emergent.
However, there are Next Economy principles that you can use to
guide your efforts to start, grow, and develop organizations that deliver
needed goods and services to your community in ways that benefit all life.

The following principles are guideposts, rather than static,
unchanging truths. In working with more than 300 social enterprises
over the past decade, we have found these principles to be highly
useful in directing your attention and energies to creating a world that
works for all life, with no one left behind. We have modified them over
the years, and they have been deeply informed by feedback from our
growing Next Economy MBA alumni community. We have also not yet
found an existing organization that is fully expressing all ten of these
principles to the degree that we feel is needed to truly shift the global
economic system.

1. Meet Basic Needs

We believe in meeting basic human needs first. As mentioned earlier,
these basic needs include, but are not limited to, nourishing food,
clean water, clean air, access to education, access to medicine, clothing, shelter, and safety. The BAU economy—as evidenced by the rates
of malnutrition, houselessness, and lack of access to clean water—is

not meeting human needs equitably. Creating a caring economy that addresses basic needs and reduces suffering is possible.

Buckminster Fuller, a renowned 20th-century inventor and visionary, once issued a mandate to humanity: "Make the world work, for 100% of humanity, in the shortest possible time, through spontaneous cooperation, without ecological offense or the disadvantage of anyone."[13] This principle is our attempt to encapsulate Fuller's call to action.

Entrepreneurs who prioritize providing goods and services that address basic needs are directly challenging the BAU economy. The late legal activist Edgar Cahn explained in *No More Throwaway People* that the current economy is designed to fulfill human greed, not human need. Cahn observed that "between 80 and 90% of all the money made in the world has nothing to do with producing goods or services or buying capital equipment to produce goods or services. It is money making money off of money. Some have said: it is money delinked from value."[14]

Being need-oriented tasks you with providing human-centered essentials in a way that does not diminish the ability to survive and thrive—in other words, without destroying habitat and ecosystems to source materials for food, clothing, shelter, and transportation infrastructure. This principle also asks you to consider ecosystem repair (aquifer recharge, improved soil fertility, habitat for wildlife, etc.) as impact outcomes of your business functions.

One example to help illustrate this principle is from the Multicultural Refugee Coalition in Austin, Texas. MRC Austin was founded in 2008 by Next Economy MBA graduate Meg Erskine. At the time, Meg was working with refugees and began to notice that many of the skills they brought from their lived experiences—such as growing food and sewing clothing—were marginalized and disregarded by the BAU economy. In addition, because of systemic racism and prejudice against immigrants, the immigrant population in her community was struggling to access job security and financial stability. She founded MRC Austin to change the narrative, building cross-racial solidarity and supporting immigrants to build dignified, fair-wage livelihoods that embrace the incredible skills they brought with them along with their cultures, stories, and worldviews.

Today, MRC Austin has created Open Arms Studio, a textile manufacturer that provides advanced sewing training and fair-wage employment for refugees, and New Leaf Agriculture, a 20-acre organic farm and community garden that connects refugees to sustainable farming opportunities. We love this example of an enterprise that prioritizes meeting the basic needs of immigrants. We also love that this population is producing basic goods such as food and clothing for themselves and others in the surrounding community.

2. Share Ownership

Sharing ownership seeks to ensure that people of color, women, folks with disabilities, immigrants, and other traditionally underrepresented groups benefit from the ownership of their ideas and labor. This is no small undertaking as white, cisgender, heterosexual, affluent, able-bodied men are often concentrated at the top of many systems. Sharing ownership as a principle of organizational design can force you to confront these systems and lead you to creatively explore how to explicitly build cross-racial, multi-gendered, and multicultural models of ownership.

But what does sharing ownership actually look like? The East Bay Permanent Real Estate Cooperative (EBPREC) is a great example of an entity that is revolutionizing the way housing is done in this country. EBPREC also exemplifies diverse, equitable, and inclusive ownership. This social enterprise, incorporated as a California Cooperative Corporation in 2017, is a Black- and Indigenous-led, multi-stakeholder cooperative with a mission to create pathways for everyday people to organize, finance, acquire, and co-steward land and housing. Ownership is divided across four key stakeholder groups comprising diverse backgrounds: tenant-owners, staff-owners, community-owners, and investor-owners. Among other things, EBPREC is showing how to open ownership opportunities and build wealth for traditionally disenfranchised groups.

Another leading example of diverse and inclusive ownership is the Boston Ujima Project. The Ujima Project is organizing neighbors, workers, business owners, and investors to create a community-controlled economy in Greater Boston. The project particularly focuses on supporting communities of color, and seeks to create a new business and finance ecosystem that democratizes local investment, production, and consumption to grow community wealth and resilience. The project is in the process of building and connecting a democratic investment and real estate fund, a business alliance that meets community standards, a worker council, and an alternative local currency.

A governing body of members (working-class Boston residents, small-business owners, activists, and investors) votes on which businesses and resources they want to see in their communities, as well as which businesses to invest in. Boston residents who do not identify as working class or a person of color can join as a solidarity member. Businesses being considered for investment are held to community standards designed by members, such as allowing workers to complete a yearly workers' satisfaction survey, employing at least 60 percent people of color, and demonstrating commitment to a green energy plan and zero waste plan.

3. Democratize Governance

There are compelling reasons to develop an equitable and democratic culture in your organization. Creating explicitly nonhierarchical, democratic, and inclusive culture is a long journey, but we have found it to be one that is deeply rewarding and critical to a future that works for everyone.

The staff of any entity are the sensors and actors in the system. When they are directly involved in decision-making, they are more likely to support implementation—even if they hold differing opinions and positions. When you engage and trust staff you can delegate more authority to everyone in the organization. Though it may take longer—especially if you have to train folks who are new to being democratically empowered—it will eventually lead to more stable governance and organizational longevity.

In this context, democracy is a living practice to be exercised, evolved, and refined over time. This is in contrast to the stagnant governance seen in some democratic countries where citizens have the right to vote once a year or so, but many actually do not. Democracy is a muscle that needs to be activated and exercised in order to avoid atrophying. Can you imagine the impact of experiencing democratic empowerment 365 days per year rather than just one single day? It can be very powerful.

This principle can manifest in many ways. Democratic organizations are like snowflakes: they are all beautiful and no two are identical. They each have their own unique expression. Some organizations may be small and flat: every member has an equal vote and individuals have delegated authority to make decisions in their area of responsibility. Some organizations may be large and layered, with much of the governance delegated to a board of directors or a general manager who is elected and beholden to the larger membership.

In some ways, even more radical than the directly democratic organizations are the self-managing organizations, where authority is more or less more completely delegated. Individuals may be invited to create their own job descriptions and set their own salaries and can make high-level decisions through a process of seeking advice from those who are impacted or have experience in the matter. The book *Reinventing Organizations: A Guide to Creating Organizations Inspired by the Next Stage in Human Consciousness* by Frederic Laloux[15] is a great resource for anyone interested in learning more about self-managing organizations.

4. Support Local Communities

The overcentralization and concentration of the BAU economy has separated the point of consumption far from the point of production. This makes the BAU economy incredibly fragile—the antithesis of a resilient, local living economy. As an example, the global supply-chain crisis that started at the beginning of the COVID pandemic in 2020 has shown how vulnerable the economy is to disruption.

The benefits of moving spending and deposits locally can be significant. Many studies demonstrate that local businesses tend to support other local businesses (via supplies, services, taxes, etc.).[16] The

American Independent Business Alliance compiled studies to find that national chain retail stores invest only 13.6 percent of assets back into the community compared to 48 percent by independents.[17] Authors Michael H. Shuman (*Put Your Money Where Your Life Is*, Berrett-Koehler, 2020) and Stacey Mitchell (*Big-Box Swindle*, 2006) have written about this "multiplier effect" extensively.

Moving deposits from large corporate banks to local credit unions and community banks is also important. Since 1994, the assets of large banks have ballooned from 9 percent of the share of U.S. Deposits to now having more than 53 percent of the market.[18] Many mission-driven businesses, cooperatives, and nonprofits are customers of some of the largest banks. Sometimes this is because large banks provide services that are not available elsewhere. For example, a local grocery store may need a bank that can provide coins and other hard currency to refill the cash registers each night (a service that many small banks and credit unions do not provide). However, many mission-driven businesses have never considered switching away from the large banks. Shifting these deposits to community banks and credit unions could produce a multibillion-dollar reinvestment strategy in local communities. Local banks tend to lend locally. In 2018, even though community-based financial institutions held just 16 percent of the market share, they still made 52 percent of all small-business lending.[19]

Many communities have also used the tools of coinvestment and local currency to keep investment dollars circulating locally. One successful example is the Bangla-Pesa, an alternative currency created in Kenya to weather times when communities are financially poor yet still have resources like food and supplies that they can transact. Another is BerkShares, an alternative currency based in the Berkshire region of western Massachusetts that has kept more than $10 million in local circulation instead of "leaking" outside the area.[20]

Many communities have innovative strategies for supporting local economic ecosystems. One is the Cecosesola cooperative, founded in Venezuela in 1967, which offers opportunities to secure food and healthcare. Cecosesola's cooperatively structured enterprises have been able to reduce the cost of food and healthcare offerings between 30 and 60 percent compared to privately operated markets. By having a robust culture of cooperation where 1,300 members (and the 60,000 Venezuelans who procure food at the weekly markets) understand the value of supporting a local economy ecosystem, Cecosesola has been able to ensure affordable access to essential human needs.[21]

Another example is Cooperation Jackson, based in Jackson, Mississippi. The organization is the realization of a vision decades in the making, inspired by generations of Black cooperative history in the South, rooted deep within the struggle for democratic rights, economic justice, self-determination, and dignity for all workers. The organizers behind Cooperation Jackson believe that a solidarity economy rooted in democratic principles is a core requirement for developing the community's capacity to make meaningful change.

Several cooperatives already exist as part of the Cooperation Jackson network. These include The Green Team lawn care business, Freedom Farms organic vegetable farm, The Center for Community Production print shop and 3D printer, and the Balagoon Center cooperative incubator. Cooperation Jackson also owns about three hectares of land which it operates as a community land trust.

While it will undoubtedly take years, if not decades, the founders of Cooperation Jackson believe the organization has the potential to achieve the size and beneficial impacts of large cooperative networks like Mondragón in the Basque region of Spain or Emilia-Romagna in Italy and in the process transform the lives of working-class Jacksonians.

5. Integrate Education

One of the trends we want to reverse on the pathway to an economy that works for all life is overspecialization of society into producer and consumer groups. We want to encourage and empower so-called consumers to become their own producers. One way to do this is to embed education of how to do or make something into the product or service so folks have the option to do it themselves. It is a myth that people do not want to work with their hands or do labor for themselves. It may be true that long periods of hard, physical labor are not for everyone, but there can be profound satisfaction in using your own hands to meet your own needs. We see many people eager for hands-on engagement in their daily lives. If producers include education as part of their offering, it gives people the knowledge to meet more of their own needs and brings the satisfaction and security of providing for themself and their community.

This would help us shift away from an extractive economy where the means of production are owned by large institutions or factories and are inaccessible to regular people. Instead, we would deploy a solution and share it so everyone can meet that need reliably. This in turn would allow you to move on to solving the next set of problems.

One example of this principle is at the company All Power Labs, which makes gasification machines that turn biomass into electricity and produce hot water and biochar. Their product replaces diesel generators at a much lower environmental cost. In addition to selling the finished product, they sell gasification kits and maintain a webpage to share instructions, resources, and results from other projects to benefit the field as a whole. This gives people the option to buy the finished product or to build it themselves.

Another great example of this principle in action is at the nonprofit GreenWave, whose mission is to help build a regenerative ocean farming industry as an emergency response to climate change. GreenWave's polyculture farming system grows a mix of seaweeds and shellfish that require no artificial inputs, while simultaneously sequestering carbon and rebuilding reef ecosystems. This is a very sustainable form of food production. GreenWave is able to produce high yields with a small footprint because their farms sit vertically below the ocean surface. The system has a relatively low barrier to entry, so anyone with access to 20 acres of ocean, a boat, and $20,000 to $50,000 can start their own farm. The company makes their model of ocean farming open to all, providing farmer training, tools, and a community of practice to support the collective growth of this important movement. GreenWave is also actively helping build markets for farmed products.

6. Promote Open Source

Open sourcing and regional replication are critical to getting to a future vision of an economy that works for the benefit of all life. One of the biggest shifts that society needs to make is to move away from the BAU concept of intellectual property. The current dominant U.S. business paradigm is leveraging intellectual property for outsized return or wealth accumulation—for example, the enormous corporate profits from developing the COVID vaccines.

But if a process or solution is working, and meeting human needs, this can be an intellectual contribution to humanity. Open source enables all of humanity to leverage those ideas for the good of humanity and also acknowledges that production is not only an individual effort. Even if you are alone in a room writing a novel, you are leaning on the resources, learning, and support of the family or community that raised you, language that you inherited, and school system that contributed to your education. All these things make it possible to do your work.

When we discuss open source, this does not necessarily mean "free." Nor does it mean that ideas should be freely used without appropriate credit and acknowledgment of origins. Attribution matters. Marginalized identities have been and continue to be discredited and ignored for the contributions made to society. For example, macaroni and cheese was popularized in America by James Hemings, who was enslaved by Thomas Jefferson. Neither Hemings nor his descendants have earned any royalties from the Kraft company. Cultural appropriation of Black and Indigenous cultures and lifeways is frequent in the current economy. Attribution and acknowledgment and generous compensation to BIPOC folks is one way to fight against this historical pattern.

Regional replication is another key component of this principle. The BAU approach to addressing market opportunities is often to seek "rapid scaling," where one company grows larger and larger to capture as much of the market as possible for monopoly control and earnings or perceived value maximization. Think of the hype around finding the next startup "unicorn." That type of scaling does not need to be the only way to achieve success in meeting everyone's needs. Global challenges can be solved, not by scaling one company larger, but by

1. Open sourcing the information
2. Ensuring the products/services and organizational models are regionally adapted
3. Achieving growth by regional and/or local economies of scale

An example of this is the Alcoholics Anonymous (AA) movement, which open sources the method of overcoming addiction in a way that allows chapters to easily replicate these community-based self-help approaches for a place-based approach. Replication and sharing of information reduce the need to create more funds to "purchase" or acquire knowledge. This is different from franchising, where instead of sharing you have individual ownership of franchises with very centralized growth, centralized market research (often done by corporate headquarters), and concentration of wealth into one company and owners of different franchises.

An innovative example of regional replication is the Evergreen Cooperatives, which are modeled on the highly successful Mondragón Corporation in the Basque region of Spain. The Evergreen Cooperative Initiative (launched in 2009 by the Cleveland Foundation, with the support of the Ohio Employee Ownership Center and the Democracy Collaborative) has created living-wage jobs in Cleveland's University Circle neighborhood, where the median household income is below $18,500 and unemployment is as high as 30 percent. Instead of offering incentives for corporations to bring what are often low-wage jobs into the city, the Evergreen strategy creates new employee-owned businesses. Through the strategy (also known as "the Cleveland Model") of tapping into the supply chains of large anchor institutions, Evergreen first creates jobs, and then recruits and trains local worker-owners to run the new companies. Evergreen launched with a commercial laundry service, solar installation, and indoor urban farming as a nested group of cooperatives supported by a shared back office that also offers business support services.

As of 2021 Evergreen had created 320 high-quality jobs and 85 worker-owners who each get a share of the profits and participate in decision-making.[22] Evergreen has since added the Fund for Employee Ownership, which acquires small- to medium-size local businesses from retiring owners and converts them to employee-owned businesses. It already supports four converted businesses alongside the existing cooperatives. The Evergreen Cooperatives were designed to be a model for reviving economically depressed urban centers that could be emulated in other U.S. cities. To date, there have been formal regional replication feasibility studies conducted in Rochester, New York, and Richmond, Virginia.

7. Embody Transparency

There is a story in the mythology of BAU capitalism that only certain exceptionally intelligent, talented, and ambitious people have the acumen to make important decisions (such as CEOs and their executive teams). The problem is that this belief results in forgoing the direct experience and intelligence of those who are closest to the implementation of certain decisions. By restricting staff from governing the affairs of their direct operations, the organization risks not only poor decision-making and results, but also the demoralization and lack of motivation that go along with it.

In organizations that truly embody the principle of transparency, however, we see staff respond to the trust and honesty of shared information with increased engagement, enthusiasm, and professional competency (for more information, see the research of Robert Kegan, Lisa Lahey, Andy Fleming, and Matthew Miller on Deliberately Developmental Organizations).[23] Instead of relying only on top executives, you can have a much larger set of eyes, minds, and collective intelligence available to address challenges. The team gets to build trust, connection, and skill at collaborative problem-solving and decision-making as common behaviors to lead the company forward. This is not always easy to do. It can require careful recruiting, expectation setting, and ongoing training in many areas from emotional intelligence, communication skills, conflict transformation, financial literacy, systems design, and more.

One clear example of this principle is expressed by the financial management practice known as Open-Book Management (OBM). People are highly intelligent and very capable of understanding financial matters. When your team can see how their work affects the organization's finances, they are often more intrinsically motivated to manage and improve their performance. Every adult has to manage their own personal finances and life decisions at home, and there is no reason they cannot bring this capability to work. Most people are quite capable of providing astute financial oversight and decision-making—especially when given financial literacy and management training. This does not necessarily mean that all the books are open to everyone all the time. Each team or department can have their own dashboard of metrics that their roles impact directly and have transparency and accountability for the results they create. When a company commits to this, trains staff, and empowers them, the results can outperform more traditionally managed companies.

Though we have focused on internal company transparency in this section, it applies just as well to being transparent with customers and the public. One example of this is Driftaway Coffee, based in New York City. Every Driftaway Coffee shows the price the company paid for it. The price Driftaway pays to its farmers is more than double (and often more than triple) the commodity price of coffee.

8. Regenerate Systems

All organizations in the economy interact with the environment in some way (even if indirectly by using electricity that comes from power plants) and with people in some way (employees, customers, suppliers, etc.). Each of these interactions has the potential to perpetuate harm and sustain the status quo or regenerate the life-giving capacity of place and people. It is possible to create enterprises that generate net positive benefit for people, the economy, and natural ecosystems. Instead of thinking it cannot be done, you can use this principle as a systems design lens to search for and select strategies that create net positive social and environmental impact.

Look at every element of your organization and only consider assets or processes that contribute to environmental and community health. If you need a raw good for your supply, source it from a producer who uses regenerative growing methods that enhance biodiversity, restore watersheds, and increase soil fertility. If you have a building in your operation, you can retrofit or design the building to use carbon sequestering materials in its construction, catch and sequester stormwater, provide habitat in living walls and green roofs, produce more energy than it uses through diversified renewable sources, improve the air quality, and inspire resilience in your community.

Agriculture provides a clear picture of a system that can regenerate itself. For example, land is cultivated to grow crops, crops are processed into food (with waste being composted back into soil), and food is digested into manure (and added back to the soil), thereby ensuring soil fertility and abundant future harvests. This type of circular, regenerative cycle can be seen in other sectors of the economy where materials or resources are used to create some benefit and then can be cycled back into their original state to create more.

Another example of this principle in action is at the Omega Center for Sustainable Living (OSCL) in upstate New York. Omega Institute is an educational organization dedicated to holistic studies, offering workshops, retreats, and conferences on its 250-acre site that hosts more than 20,000 people a year. The OSCL features an Eco Machine that processes all the wastewater generated on-site in an all-natural closed-loop system. This basic function is a remarkable improvement over conventional systems that use chemicals, energy, and waste. It is also a beautiful system that features an aerated lagoon and constructed wetlands using living plants to purify water in a building that also hosts workshops and tours. Abundance, deeper connection, and cascading benefits are often the result of designing for the whole system.

Another example is Sustainable Organic Integrated Livelihoods (SOIL) Haiti, a social enterprise that has responded to the health crisis of inadequate sanitation in Haiti's urban areas through ecological sanitation. They distribute composting toilets, collect the waste, and process it into nutrient-dense organic compost to be used to grow food and reforest the island. During the recent political unrest, violence, and acute humanitarian emergency, SOIL Haiti has, against all odds, continued to provide weekly sanitation service to over 2,000 households subscribed to their EkoLakay waste collection service.

9. Develop People

Imagine if your workplace constantly encouraged your personal growth and development. Imagine if it were a place where you could practice new skills, learn about the world, and learn about yourself. Your job requirements, in addition to your organization roles, would include advancing your health, addressing your trauma, learning how to be a good community member, identifying how to help society, and learning how to grow spiritually. In this workplace, instead of performance reviews, you could have collaborative performance enhancement support, where team members serve as coaches and enthusiastic supporters invested in each person's advancement and fulfillment. There would be ongoing investment in team culture to boost morale and enthusiasm.

This radical opportunity for personal growth within organizations has been validated by many, including Robert Kegan and Lisa Lahey from Harvard in their book, *An Everyone Culture: Becoming a Deliberately Developmental Organization*. Kegan and Lahey observed organizational cultures that were both empowering and demanding in their commitment to personal growth. One key insight from Kegan and Lahey's work is that everyone must practice growth and development for DDOs to work. This collectively agreed-upon, aspirational culture creates the container to hold oneself and one's teammates to a higher standard of development and performance that is unparalleled in traditional management environments.

We have seen this principle in action at a number of organizations, for example, global tech cooperative CoLab Cooperative. CoLab would arrange a paid weekly mindfulness session while also actively investing in mediation and nonviolent communication (NVC) training for member-owners. World Centric, a B Corp that develops compostable food containers and donates a significant portion of profits to alleviating suffering in the world, hosts regular lunch-and-learns to provide in-depth, all-hands learning on diverse topics such as ocean health, food security, civic engagement, and more.

This may seem "too expensive" or "too wishy-washy" to be a viable business practice. However, if you think about it as a long-term investment, you can imagine a team culture that supports each individual in their personal growth and development. Individuals who are focused, inspired, and rooted in a deep sense of purpose will bring their best selves to their work. This provides the foundation for an aspirational team culture that can create meaningful and sustained positive impact in the world.

10. Build Movements

While the previous principles may be impactful and inspiring, they are, by themselves, insufficient to create the transformation needed to achieve collective liberation. The Center for Racial Justice in Education defines collective liberation this way:

> *Collective liberation acknowledges that multiple oppressions exist, and that we work in solidarity to undo oppression in ourselves, our families, our communities, and our institutions, in order to achieve a world that is truly free. We work collectively because we recognize that each of us has a stake in ending white supremacy and all related systems of oppression. Collective liberation requires that we center the voices and lived experiences of those who have been most marginalized. Collective liberation is found in community and relationship building, and in the sharing of our stories, including our sorrow and our joy. Collective liberation depends on our communities to build shared power and accountability that foster a just and transformed world.*[24]

Achieving this goal requires widespread cooperation and solution sharing in addition to many small-scale solutions. Movements that challenge the structural components of society through actions that change policies, undermine and disrupt unjust laws, and bring new civic technologies into practice are also needed. It is not enough to be independently successful in a convergence of crises. Resilience requires interdependence.

A number of movement-building organizations, including Movement for Black Lives, New Economy Coalition, and Wellbeing Economy Alliance, have crafted policy platforms with a diverse set of recommendations that Next Economy organizations could align and organize around:

- *Overhaul the justice system to a transformative justice model.* Transformative justice is a political framework and approach for responding to violence, harm, and abuse. At its most basic, it seeks to respond to violence and harm without creating more violence and harm.

- *Work to elect progressive district attorneys and local representatives.*

- *Advocate for governance choice development by citizen assemblies and other public deliberative bodies.* A citizen assembly is a body formed from randomly selected citizens to deliberate on important issues and develop choices to be considered by voters.

- *Implement a three- or four-day workweek.*

- *Advocate for the creation of public banks.* A public bank is a chartered depository bank in which public funds are deposited, owned by a government unit—a state, county, city, or tribe— and mandated to serve a public mission that reflects the values and needs of the public that it represents. In the United States, North Dakota has had a public bank since 1919. Recently, New York, Washington, California, Oregon, Philadelphia, and San Francisco all introduced bills to establish or take the necessary steps toward the establishment of public banks.

- *Mandate true-cost accounting.* True-cost accounting is a method that accounts for all direct and indirect costs. Including environmental, social, and economic costs generated by the creation of a product, service, or organization.

- *Institute a land value tax.* A land value tax is a more predictable way to tax property based solely on the value of a parcel of land and not any associated buildings, personal property, or other improvements. This would provide a broad tax base because it would include all empty properties and empty sites (as opposed to only taxing property with buildings). Many argue that a land value tax would reduce urban sprawl, encourage the use of empty sites, and encourage a shift of private investment from land speculation (which creates no extra land but only higher land prices) to more productive uses of the land.

- *Implement universal basic income or unconditional cash transfers.*

- *Create a universal employment guarantee.* This would provide a good job to every person who wants one—permanently enshrining the right to dignified work as a fundamental human right.

- *Implement restrictions on multinational franchise activity.* This prevents or limits local resources from leaving the community to benefit owners who live outside the area.

- *Enact a diversity of reparations strategies.* No single reparation strategy or approach will be right for all communities. We need to explore a diversity of approaches.

- *Advocate for land-back policies.* Restore stolen lands to Indigenous peoples, particularly lands that are currently under government control. For example, the City of Oakland announced plans in 2022 to return approximately five acres of city-owned land to Indigenous stewardship.

- *Support the rights of nature.* This is a legal theory that describes inherent rights associated with ecosystems and species, similar to the concept of fundamental human rights. Ecuador and Bolivia are examples of countries that have adopted the rights of nature in their constitutions.

- *Institute public procurement policies that privilege Next Economy organizations.*

Movement Generation Justice and Ecology Project provides a focused strategic approach in the five pillars of their Just Transition framework. These include advancing ecological restoration; democratizing communities, wealth, and the workplace; driving racial justice and social equity; relocalizing most production and consumption; and retaining and restoring cultures and traditions. The exploration of each pillar could fill volumes, but the point is that no one entity or organization can achieve these goals alone. They are imperatives for humankind as a whole. While many organizations are making progress in these areas through their work towards their own vision, our emphasis is on the wider network of collaboration. Imagine if every small business or organization were using their resources not just independently but contributing them together to propel collective movements.

One example of movement building is the founding of the United States Federation of Worker Cooperatives (USFWC) in 2004. At the time there were cooperative networks in the San Francisco Bay Area and a few other local areas like Madison, Wisconsin, and Portland, Oregon. There were also separate West Coast and East Coast cooperative conferences but no formal national organization. Organizers founded the USFWC in order to promote democracy in the workplace at a broader level. The USFWC provides support to about 1,000 democratic organizations by helping new co-ops start, providing technical assistance, advocating for policy changes, providing collective benefits, and helping with fundraising. Though the scale of their work is still small, it represents greater capacity than the individual member organizations would have on their own. We believe this pattern of organizations doing good work in their own spheres of influence and then collaborating across networks to deploy solutions at wider scales is critical to creating meaningful change.

Another example is the American Sustainable Business Network (ASBN). ASBN is a movement builder in partnership with the business and investor community. ASBN develops and advocates solutions for policymakers, business leaders, and investors that support an equitable, regenerative, and just economy that benefits people and the planet. As a multi-issue membership organization advocating on behalf of every business sector, size, and geography, ASBN and its association members collectively represent more than 250,000 businesses across its networks.

How Is It Possible to Do All of These?!

If you are feeling overwhelmed by the prospect of integrating these principles, don't worry. As mentioned previously, no organization we have encountered is fully expressing all 10 principles at once. We hope that by identifying and describing them above, we are inviting Next Economy organizations to invest in creative ways to further integrate and express these principles as a means of leading society towards a better future.

The Price Parity Paradox

The price parity paradox (or PPP) is one major barrier Next Economy enterprises face in integrating these principles more deeply. The PPP is when the good or service with the lowest price (often achieved through exploitation of people and planet) has a significant advantage over the higher-priced Next Economy good or service. The cost reductions that companies achieve when they acquire lower-cost goods by exploiting people and the planet result in effects called "externalities," because the actual costs (to communities and the biosphere) are accounted for external to the company and not factored into their balance sheet.

"True-cost accounting," as mentioned in Principle 10: Build Movements, describes an approach that seeks to accurately reflect all the costs incurred in the business undertakings. However, true-cost accounting is not a universally applied standard and most companies have not adopted the practice. Next Economy organizations may find it difficult to achieve price parity (charge roughly the same amount for their goods and services) with their BAU competitors. It can even seem like a contradiction for Next Economy organizations to seek to charge the same as their BAU competitors.

In addition, adopting and applying all 10 principles of Next Economy enterprises will likely result in a higher cost of production when compared to BAU goods or services. This implies that the price charged to consumers will need to be higher. This premium price may create accessibility barriers for many communities, such as low-income communities, that need these goods or services. Instead, folks from privileged communities who have surplus capital are more likely able to afford the price premium.

There are ways to deliver these goods or services that counteract the price advantage enjoyed by BAU goods and services. The methods we have seen Next Economy organizations use to address the PPP include "demand side" approaches (increasing consumer demand for your products) and "supply side" approaches (creating new revenue-generating opportunities or efficiencies that lower the cost to produce goods or services). These are some of the demand side approaches:

- *Make your customers your owners.* Creating a cooperative—such as a consumer cooperative like Recreational Equipment Inc. (REI)—makes your customers your owners. Your customers may be willing to spend more (when possible) for your goods and services if they benefit from any profits generated. This does not work when customers do not have the ability to afford a premium price.

- *Differentiate pricing for different markets in creative ways.* Try to experiment with sliding-scale, values-based invoicing, and different pricing for different markets. For example, Everytable in Los Angeles offers differentiated pricing for the same entree—higher price in the more affluent parts of the city and lower price in those harder-hit by racialized capitalism—in an effort to make high-quality nutritious food affordable to all.

- *Transparency.* Sharing the true cost of products can motivate certain customers to pay the premium when they can. Everytable has a "pay it forward" option for folks who have surplus to support folks who do not have access to healthy food.

- *Philanthropic subsidy.* Find philanthropic support or other charitable resources to reduce the price of goods to certain populations. This can work, but it can be difficult to sustain over long periods of time.

In contrast, here are some of the supply-side strategies to increase revenue-generating opportunities or reduce the cost of providing your goods and services:

- *Advocate for true-cost accounting.* At the policy level, you can advocate for eliminating subsidies for BAU enterprises and creating structural ways to enforce true-cost accounting (including externalities that have a long time horizon such as climate change and climate change risk) that can help even the playing field for Next Economy businesses.

- *Cooperatively reduce the cost of raw materials.* Building partnerships with values-aligned organizations can help reduce the price of providing Next Economy goods or services. For more on this topic, see the "Strategic Partnerships" section in "Part 7: Strategy."

- *Vertically integrate.* Vertical integration is when a company develops ownership over aspects of its supply chain that were previously subcontracted to external suppliers. This can offer substantial cost savings through efficiencies of scale.

- *Cooperate efficiently.* In a nonhierarchical, self-managed cooperative, salary for management labor is not needed. For more, see the "Decision-Making and Governance" section in "Part 7: Strategy."

- *Increase worker-ownership.* Worker-ownership can reduce expenses because it typically eliminates the premiums paid to shareholders or highly compensated executives. Taking management and shareholder profit out of enterprise costs can sometimes decrease costs enough to approach price parity. There can also be a different motivation to produce surplus because, depending on the cooperative's particular situation and priorities, workers typically take home some (or all) of the profits.

- *Reduce salary expense through creative total compensation.* In some cases, workers might value benefits like flexibility, caring work culture, and opportunities for personal growth and accept lower wages in exchange.

- *Innovate.* Many innovations could be helpful on this journey to achieve cost reductions. For example, business model innovations such as moving from a sales model to a "goods as a service" model can address the waste-producing aspects of the economy. It creates a more circular economy approach where consumers pay not for the ownership of a good, but for the service of using it until the point where they no longer need the good, or the good is in need of repair, at which point it is returned to the company for refurbishment and passed onto the next user. Another innovation to consider is coproduct development. The production of many goods yields additional products that also have beneficial uses (coproducts) but that often get wasted. Seeking to capture these and sell them as coproducts can add revenue-generating sources. For example, in the case of wool, a few potential co-products are lanolin (an oil in sheep's wool that is highly beneficial for skin care) and wool short fibers and dust that could have applications for bioplastics and the 3D printing space.

The PPP is called a paradox because it is difficult to navigate and there are no simple answers. Competing with the BAU economy often requires financial and structural gymnastics. We hope this incomplete list of approaches provides a rough roadmap to help you with experimentation, organizational design, and value proposition development.

Finally, it should be noted that the PPP will never be fully resolved until there is a functioning regulatory apparatus (that is not captured by corporations) to regulate poor behavior out of existence. Ultimately we need to have corporations internalize the cost. If they did, it would be much cheaper to get your clothes from a bioregional producer that benefits people and the planet. This is because—from a true-cost accounting perspective—clothing made by a BAU company would actually be more expensive.

3

Enterprise Structures and Legal Frameworks

Implementing the principles in "Part 2: Principles of Next Economy Enterprises" is not enough to transition to the Next Economy. The BAU economy has operating structures and legal systems that favor the status quo and suppress change. Thankfully, people have been working on building new structures and hacking old structures in order to change their operating systems. What structures are available? Which ones will allow your organization to best express Next Economy principles?

Structure Literacy

Many early-stage entrepreneurs fixate on the question of what legal structure they should choose in order to form their new entity. It is often one of the first questions asked. We have seen many teams put lots of energy into making the "best" decision on this. We acknowledge that it is a real decision that you will have to make and there are advantages and disadvantages to the options. We want to caution you to not conflate your organization's legal structure with its ability to succeed. The "right" structure will not determine your success, but certain structures can enable you to more easily and more reliably create the beneficial impacts you want to see in the world. Rather than expending hefty sums of time and capital on elaborate entity structure questions, we advocate for that energy to first be spent on imperative business model questions.

You should also seek to fit any of the legal structuring options to the vision and purpose of your organization—not the other way around. Focus on what is uniquely important about your organization's vision and impact in the world and how that business model can or could work. Then structure your legal entity to support that reality and do not get caught in the traps of "how this is usually done."

Finally, it is important to link your social enterprise to community stakeholders. It is very easy to deceive yourself into thinking that you are making a difference in the world. Having stakeholders involved can mitigate against these "savior" impulses.

Case Study: Sustainable Economies Law Center (SELC) THESELC.ORG

Founded in 2009 by Janelle Orsi and Jenny Kassan in Oakland, California, the Sustainable Economies Law Center is a nonprofit 501(c)(3) organization that seeks to cultivate a new legal landscape that supports community resilience and grassroots economic empowerment. SELC recognizes and provides resources and education on understanding how laws and the legal system coevolved with the BAU economy (encoding and presupposing relationships like landlord/tenant, employer/employee, and similar, often exploitative or asymmetric, relationships). These systems are inadequate and are in need of transformation to enable the Next Economy. SELC operates nearly a dozen programs for education, research, advocacy, and advice and creates free and accessible tools and templates so communities everywhere can develop their own sustainable sources of food, housing, energy, jobs, and other vital aspects of a thriving community.

NEXT ECONOMY PRINCIPLES REPRESENTED:

- 1 Meet Basic Needs
- 2 Share Ownership
- 3 Democratize Governance

(continued)

Case Study: Sustainable Economies Law Center (SELC) *(continued)*

- 4 Support Local Communities
- 5 Integrate Education
- 6 Promote Open Source
- 7 Embody Transparency
- 9 Develop People
- 10 Build Movements

One last consideration is to differentiate between legal structure and operational structure. Your legal structure is the entity registered with the state government. Your operational structure includes governance strategies, tactics, and how you organize your staff in different departments and individual roles. As our friends at the Sustainable Economies Law Center (SELC) have documented in their model of worker self-directed nonprofits, nonprofits can be governed democratically, similar to worker-owned cooperatives, through a creative combination of the following:

- Time-limited board resolutions that delegate management functions to the nonprofit staff
- Creating board seats for workers, subject to any limitations that the state of incorporation might have regarding "financially interested" directors
- Provisions within the articles of incorporation or bylaws that empower worker self-direction, subject to oversight by the board of directors
- Written policies adopted by the board of directors that further define the process of worker self-direction

Now we'll look at some of the various options for legal entity structuring, some tax designations, and some other terms that are sometimes conflated with legal entities.

Unincorporated Association

Your business needs to be registered as a legal entity in many instances. However, in some circumstances no legal structure at all may be appropriate for the vision as a whole or during a certain stage of development. If your project has no or very low revenue or is using nonfinancial reciprocity such as gift, barter, or exchange, you may be fine to remain unincorporated. The reasons to avoid incorporation would be to keep resources focused on the impact of the project rather than administration of the project. Incorporating your entity will involve some level of paperwork and fees and reporting to the Internal Revenue Service (IRS). If you believe you do not need the legal status, then some of this administrative burden can be limited or avoided.

Sole Proprietorship and Partnership

Oftentimes, the easiest way to start your enterprise is as a sole proprietorship. It can be as simple as filing a Schedule C form with the IRS with your income tax return. In many cases you will need to pay a business license fee as a sole proprietor to a local municipality and possibly file a fictitious business name statement. The business by default will use your Social Security Number, or you can register an Employer Identification Number (EIN) with the IRS. Partnerships are almost as simple but require two or more partners as owners of the business. In both cases the owners are directly liable for the actions associated with the business and do not have any degree of protection from claims against the business.

Limited Liability Company

A Limited Liability Company (LLC) is a flexible legal entity that functions like a partnership with some added liability protection. Individual partners can still be subject to liability. It does cost more than a partnership or sole proprietorship with many states charging an annual fee.

Corporation

The vast majority of publicly traded companies—Apple, Nike, Tesla— are incorporated as Corporations and taxed under subchapter C. This entity type offers protection from personal liability for individuals. It can be complicated to set up and is commonly incorporated by attorneys. It also often carries an annual fee.

S Corporation

An S corporation elects to be taxed under a special tax designation where earnings are not taxed at the federal level but pass through as taxable income for the owners (whether the earnings are disbursed as actual dividends or distributions or not at all). Distributions to shareholders are not subject to payroll tax (although shareholders who work for the business must pay themselves primarily in salary, which is subject to payroll tax). The individual owners will still have to declare the income and pay individual income tax.

Benefit Corporation

A benefit corporation is a legal entity that helps to create a solid foundation for long-term mission alignment and value creation. Directors of traditional for-profit companies (especially publicly traded companies) often face extreme pressure to maximize financial returns to shareholders. This singular focus is called "shareholder primacy." This can make it very difficult for companies to prioritize their social and environmental mission. Becoming a benefit corporation gives a company legal permission to consider anyone that is materially affected by that company's decision-making, such as workers, customers, local communities, and the environment. As of 2022, 38 states in the United States have benefit corporation statutes. Internationally Italy, Colombia, and Ecuador have statutes currently and Argentina, Australia, Canada, and Chile are in the works.

Certified B Corporation

A Certified B Corporation (B Corp) is not a legal entity structure. B Corps are companies that have been certified by the nonprofit B Lab to have met rigorous standards of social and environmental performance, accountability, and transparency. B Corp certification is similar to Leadership in Energy and Environmental Design (LEED) certification for green buildings, Fairtrade certification for coffee, or USDA Organic certification for produce. A key difference, however, is that B Corp certification looks at an entire company and its practices (such as worker engagement, community involvement, environmental footprint, governance structure, and customer relationships) rather than just one aspect, such as the building or a product. Today, a growing global community of thousands of Certified B Corporations across hundreds of industries are helping to redefine success in business.

Case Study: World Centric   WORLDCENTRIC.COM

Aseem Das launched World Centric in Palo Alto, California, as a nonprofit to raise awareness of large-scale humanitarian and environmental issues. He could not tolerate the fact that billions of people live on less than two dollars a day, without basic necessities like adequate food, water, healthcare, education, housing, and sanitation. He started by hosting documentaries and speakers on environmental, social, human rights, and peace issues. World Centric observed that if they began selling Fairtrade and compostable products, they would be able to avoid taking donations or grants, and could fund the educational work via product sales. While they continued with educational services they found themselves becoming an early mover in the field of compostable service ware, netting them multimillions in sales.

Eventually, selling compostable products became the company's primary focus and it converted from a nonprofit to a for-profit social enterprise. World Centric found a values-aligned for-profit business community in the Certified B Corp movement. Since 2009, World Centric has given at least 25 percent of its profits to grassroots social and environmental organizations, offered discounts to schools and nonprofits, and offset all of its carbon emissions from raw material to delivery in addition to providing a renewable alternative to single-use plastics. Over $9 million has been given to 238 projects globally as of 2022. They invest in projects with high impact addressing basic needs in communities experiencing extreme poverty with a preference for systemic approaches and local community empowerment and engagement.

(continued)

Worker Cooperatives

Worker cooperatives are organizations where workers are the members and owners of the organization. This stands in stark contrast to almost all other entity structures where workers are subordinate to owners who hold all the governance rights. There are cooperative statutes in many states in the U.S. As of 2022, there are over 1,000 worker co-ops. About 30% of those organizations are legally registered as worker cooperatives. The rest have traditional entity structures, such as an LLC, and then have their own internal cooperating agreements that provide for ownership and governance rights.

Case Study: FaSinPat

FaSinPat, formerly known as Zanon, is a worker-controlled ceramic tile factory in southern Argentina, and one of the most prominent and largest in the country's recovered factory movement. The name is short for Fábrica Sin Patrones (Spanish for "Factory Without Bosses"). Labor conflict with management preceded the Argentine financial collapse in 2001, when the owner fired and locked out workers. Workers then occupied the factory and resumed production in 2002 with 240 workers and became profitable.

Community relations and support sustained their takeover and subsequent success. The occupying workers without pay were initially supported by the community with donations of food. Once they resumed production, they donated tiles to community centers and hospitals

(continued)

and organized cultural activities for the community on its premises. They built a community health clinic. The workers also make monthly donations to soup kitchens and hospitals. They also developed relations with the Mapuche community to buy clay from their lands to use as raw material. They spearheaded a network of recovered enterprises, and as of 2022, more than 400 companies and more than 15,000 workers are part of the recovered-factory movement.

When production restarted under their own control, workers did not return to the days of strict obedience under the threat of being fired.

Instead, every aspect of production was revolutionized—planning, materials, safety, wages, hiring, output, and distribution were geared to the needs of the workers themselves and the wider community in which they lived. FaSinPat workers directly support their families and profits are reinvested back into the community.

NEXT ECONOMY PRINCIPLES REPRESENTED:

- 1 Meet Basic Needs
- 2 Share Ownership
- 3 Democratize Governance
- 4 Support Local Communities
- 9 Develop People
- 10 Build Movements

Producer Cooperatives

Producer cooperatives are organizations where the producers are the members and owners of the organization. This is the original cooperative structure in the United States, coming from agricultural producers. Producers of a certain commodity such as citrus fruits, cranberries, or milk pool their production together to be marketed under a common brand. You may know some of these brand names: Sunkist Citrus, Ocean Spray Cranberries, and Organic Valley. The cooperative structure allows individual producers to focus on growing or producing their product. By pooling their products and resources, the cooperative can invest in larger brand name promotion and recognition and gain wider distribution and sales.

Consumer Cooperatives

Consumer cooperatives are organizations where the consumers are the members and owners. Consumer cooperatives leverage their collective demand to buy larger amounts of products at lower prices. Some of you may be familiar with Recreational Equipment Incorporated co-op (REI) or local food co-ops. As a consumer-owner you may pay a membership fee or a labor contribution and in return get access to member pricing on groceries or recreational equipment and a vote on member issues such as electing a board of directors and other governance concerns.

Hybrid or Multi-Stakeholder Cooperatives

Hybrid or multi-stakeholder cooperatives integrate two or more classes of ownership into one organization. While still fairly new in the United States, it is exciting and promising to see entities developing that consider the governance rights of workers, consumers, and producers all at the same time. This challenges the idea that one group needs to privilege itself over the others to achieve success. Instead, each group sees itself in dynamic reciprocity with others. This creates mutually beneficial results for all stakeholders.

Case Study: Our Table Cooperative   OURTABLE.US

Our Table is a multi-stakeholder cooperative where everyone has a seat at the table, everyone gets a vote, and everyone shares in the profits. An estimated 60 percent of the owners are women and people of color. The cooperative includes a certified organic farm that practices biodynamic agriculture and a logistics operation that invites farmers from the surrounding area to store and sell their goods. The

(continued)

Case Study: Our Table Cooperative *(continued)*

facility includes cold storage, warehousing, delivery logistics, a commercial kitchen, and a retail store.

Our Table cooperative is fostering a new paradigm that brings together all stakeholders in a food value network, from farm to table, as members of a single vertically integrated cooperative:

- Worker members raise crops on the 58-acre organic farm and perform value-added processing, distribution, and retail services.

- Independent producer members allow the cooperative to scale in both product diversity and volume.

- Consumer members complete the loop by purchasing the fruits, vegetables, and other value-added goods.

NEXT PRINCIPLES REPRESENTED:

- 1 Meet Basic Needs
- 2 Share Ownership
- 3 Democratize Governance
- 4 Support Local Communities
- 9 Develop People
- 10 Build Movements

Nonprofit Organizations

Nonprofits are technically corporations that receive IRS and state designation as creating a charitable or other benefit for society. There are more than 20 nonprofit designations, but the most common is 501(c)(3), which allows the organization to offer tax deductions for qualified contributions. This is desirable as corporate and individual donors often prefer to be able to claim a charitable tax deduction on their taxes and in some cases, may require it (foundations can donate to other entity types, including for-profit businesses, provided the activities of the organization align with a charitable purpose).

Nonprofits are generally thought of as doing good work. However, the IRS's definition of "benefit" when certifying nonprofits can be dubious. For example, many 501(c)(3) "crisis pregnancy centers" are actually fake clinics designed to deter pregnant people from seeking and having an abortion. The default operational structure of many nonprofits can be very similar to traditional for-profit businesses, with governance rights concentrated on upper management levels. No ownership or equity can be offered for a nonprofit organization. Nonprofits can take on debt and can hold ownership stakes in for-profit organizations. Their annual 990 tax filings are publicly available and show important details about how much funding and assets they have, compensation of staff, and percent of budget spent on their charitable activities versus overhead.

Case Study: Homeboy Industries
HOMEBOYINDUSTRIES.ORG

Homeboy Industries, a nonprofit organization, operates over a dozen job-training social enterprise initiatives that hire and train individuals who were formerly incarcerated and/or involved in gangs. The primary goal of the organization is "to help former gang members redirect their lives and become contributing members of their families and our community." Homeboy Industries was started in 1988 by Father Gregory Boyle in the Dolores Mission Parish of East Los Angeles. The organization began as a partnership with local businesses to hire homeboy and homegirl trainees. Homeboy Industries launched a bakery, later expanded to more than a dozen other enterprises, and created a global replication program. There are now more than 400 organizations utilizing their model—making Homeboy Industries the "largest and most successful gang intervention, rehab, and re-entry program in the world."

Homeboy Industries focuses on needed goods and services such as food and recycling, now providing for community needs through Homeboy Bakery (storefront, wholesale, and online at homeboyfoods.com), Homeboy Silkscreen & Embroidery, Homegirl Café,

(continued)

Homegirl Catering, Homeboy Merchandise, farmers' markets, Homeboy Diner at Los Angeles City Hall, and Homeboy Electronics Recycling.

The enterprises generate revenue that supports the nonprofit organization to supplement grant and donation funding. Trainees are paid employees while they develop job skills and can use services provided by the nonprofit, including case management, tattoo removal, mental health services, legal services, education (academic, life skills, wellness, and enrichment classes), solar panel training and certification, and a partnership with Learning Works Charter High School. Recently, the nonprofit launched Homeboy Capital to raise philanthropic and catalytic capital to invest in early-stage enterprises with need for more workers to provide more placements for program participants, develop new enterprises from scratch to meet local economic gaps and create new jobs, acquire existing small businesses in the region, and support aligned organizations in the ecosystem through low-interest, non-extractive loan arrangements.

Homeboy Industries sees its pathway to system change through creation of high-quality jobs and training community members to be enterprise leaders through comprehensive personal growth and development cultural investments during an 18-month program. All of the personal growth and development programs and services are provided free of charge to participants. For Homeboy Industries, the nonprofit structure worked best to access the necessary philanthropic resources to catalyze the enterprise growth.

NEXT ECONOMY PRINCIPLES REPRESENTED:

- 1 Meet Basic Needs
- 2 Share Ownership
- 4 Support Local Communities
- 6 Promote Open Source
- 7 Embody Transparency
- 9 Develop People
- 10 Build Movements

Trust

A trust is a fiduciary relationship in which one party (a trustor) gives another party (the trustee) the right to hold title to property or assets for the benefit of a third party (the beneficiary). There are many different types of trust, and we will mention a few here that are currently in use in the service of Next Economy principles and projects.

A *land trust* is a legal entity that takes ownership over property for certain benefits—such as environmental conservation or to remain as agricultural land not to be developed as commercial real estate. Community land trusts hold land on behalf of a community while stewarding for affordable housing or other benefits to the community. An *employee ownership trust* (EOT), more common in European countries but now being adopted in the United States, is a legal structure that ensures that a company remains employee-owned in perpetuity. A *perpetual purpose trust* is a newer modification of the EOT, where the beneficiary is the stated purpose of the organization rather than the employees themselves. For example, Yvon Chouinard famously gave away his ownership of Patagonia, remarking "Earth is now our *only* shareholder," when he established the Patagonia Purpose Trust in 2022. For more information on perpetual purpose trusts, check out the organization Purpose US (purpose-us.com).

Case Study: Firebrand Artisan Breads
FIREBRANDBREAD.COM

Matt Kreutz grew up in the punk scene that celebrated and encouraged values of autonomy, unity, and a sense of ownership. That upbringing, plus his lived experience working in bakeries since the age of 14 and his respect for the workers involved in the craft of producing food, led him to found Firebrand Artisan Breads in 2008. Started in a warehouse in West Oakland, California, Firebrand has grown as an enterprise with a mission as "an inclusive, equitable workplace, providing good jobs for those with barriers to employment" through the

(continued)

to break the cycle of recidivism by an open hiring practice of employing formerly incarcerated and formerly unhoused team members. Employees are provided job training and supported in personal goals, such as developing financial stability and securing affordable housing. An on-site resource center offers English as a second language classes, legal and housing assistance, high school equivalency diploma classes, and other training programs.

In 2020 the organization transitioned into a steward-owned structure to encode into the charter of the corporation the purpose expressed in its practices and commitments. Aligned investors supported the transition with a $2.5 million round of financing. At the same time, Purpose US provided technical support to create Firebrand Perpetual Purpose Trust, which became the largest shareholder of the company. This non-charitable purpose trust is governed by a committee that includes Matt, employees, and community members, and is encoded in a trust document that defines the benefit of the trust as the purpose of the organization. This means the assets of the corporation must be stewarded for the benefit of the purposes Matt had baked into the DNA of the enterprise, including "protect employee and community participation in the governance of the trust and board of directors" and "prioritize hiring people who are formerly incarcerated, houseless, or otherwise have high barriers to entering the workforce."

NEXT ECONOMY PRINCIPLES REPRESENTED:

- 1 Meet Basic Needs
- 2 Share Ownership
- 3 Democratize Governance
- 7 Embody Transparency
- 9 Develop People

Employee Stock Ownership Plan

An ESOP is an employee benefit plan that awards stock shares to employees in addition to salary and other benefits. When an employee leaves the company, whether for retirement or another opportunity, they can then sell the stock back to the company for some value. The stocks convey ownership but do not bestow governance rights, though some organizations with ESOPs also give their employees these rights. Companies with ESOPs represent the largest sector of employee ownership in the United States. ESOPs are governed by the federal Employee Retirement Income Security Act of 1974 (ERISA), which can in some cases create conflict with the mission of the organization and can be expensive to establish and administer, especially for small companies (most ESOP companies have 50 or more employees).

Advantages and Disadvantages of Different Legal Structures

Each legal entity structure presents certain advantages and disadvantages. We have summarized and subjectively graded these characteristics, based on our experiences consulting with hundreds of Next Economy organizations, with a + for advantage, o for some advantage, and — for disadvantage in the chart in Figure 2.

We most frequently see Next Economy organizations choose LLC, benefit corporation, worker-owned cooperative, multi-stakeholder cooperative, or some form of nonprofit charitable corporation (with a charitable tax status like 501(c)(3) or 501(c)(4)). Here are some of the specific Next Economy advantages and drawbacks of each of these five entity types.

- **LLC**

  Advantages: LLCs offer the possibility of separating governance and economic rights of membership, allowing inclusive and equitable distribution of economic benefits (e.g., to workers or community investors) while allocating governance, voting rights, and processes to certain membership units in defined and distinct proportions to other membership units (e.g., workers can have more voting power than investors).

	Ease to Start	Cost to Start	Cost to Maintain	Liability Limitation	Flexibility	Equity Investors Allowed	Tax Complexity	"Pass-through" Tax	Can be a Certified B Corp	Democratic Governess	Inclusive Ownership	Mission Durability
Sole Proprietorship	+	+	+	—	+	—	+	+	+	O	—	—
Partnership	+	+	+	—	+	O	+	+	+	O	O	O
LLC	O	—	O	O	O	+	O	O (if "S," "K")	+	O	O	O
Benefit Corporation (L3C, PBC, etc.)	O	O	O	+	—	+	O	O (if "K")	+	O	O	O
Worker-owned Cooperative	—	—	O	+	O	—	O	+	+	+	+	O
Consumer Cooperative	—	—	O	+	O	—	O	+	+	+	+	O
Producer Cooperative	—	—	O	+	O	—	O	+	+	+	+	O
Multi-stakeholder Cooperative	—	—	O	O	O	O	O	+	+	+	+	+
Limited Cooperative Association	—	—	O	O	O	O	O	O	+	+	O	O
Perpetual Purpose Trust or other Trust-owned Structure	—	—	O	O	O	+	O	O	+	O	O	+
Nonprofit	O	—	O	+	—	—	O	+	—	O	O	+
Fiscally Sponsored Project of a Nonprofit	+	+	+	+	O	—	+	+	—	O	O	+
Key:	Advantage (+)			Some Advantage (O)			Disadvantage (—)					

FIGURE 2: Advantages and Disadvantages of Various Legal Structures
Source: Lift Economy

Disadvantages: It is often a creative enterprise for legal counsel to work with stakeholders to custom design and incorporate Next Economy principles. This can be time consuming and expensive. Also, certain investors (most institutional venture investors) will not invest in LLCs, either because of restrictions mandated by limited partner investors or due to tax and accounting compliance complexity.

- **Benefit Corporation**

  Advantages: Like LLCs, benefit corporations offer the possibility of separating governance and economic rights of membership, allowing inclusive and equitable distribution of economic benefits while governance and voting rights are differentiated among shareholders (if a benefit corporation is taxed as an S corporation it can have differentiated governance rights, but only one class of shares regarding economic rights).

  Disadvantages: It is not a guarantee that mission orientation and commitment to Next Economy principles will survive if the company is acquired or in public exchange markets if the corporation becomes publicly listed.

- **Worker-Owned Cooperative**

  Advantages: Worker-owned cooperatives can be designed to have a certain level of differentiated economic rights, but the governance rights are defined as one worker equals one vote, a construction that ensures equitable, democratic governance.

  Disadvantages: Though beneficial for workers and communities, this unique shared ownership structure has, in the past, limited cooperatives' access to outside capital. However, there is a growing set of solutions to address this challenge. These include selling preferred shares, conducting a direct public offering, and profit-sharing (a "royalty model" of payback). Each of these options are discussed in more detail in "Part 7: Strategy."

- **Multi-Stakeholder Cooperative**

  Advantages: Similar advantages to worker-owned cooperatives, with the flexibility afforded to LLCs and benefit corporations. Most multi-stakeholder cooperatives are incorporated as LLCs.

  Disadvantages: Poorly understood because multi-stakeholder co-ops are still rare in the United States, though common in places like Quebec and Italy. This makes it more difficult to find the expertise needed to create them. There are relatively few lawyers intimately familiar with establishing multi-stakeholder cooperatives.

- **Nonprofit 501(c)(3)**

  Advantages: Nonprofit corporations that have been granted tax exemption from the IRS can access charitable sources of funding that can be out of reach for organizations with for-profit structures. Nonprofit organizations can own, wholly or in part, subsidiary for-profit corporations such as a benefit corporation. With certain board resolutions, bylaws, policies, and practices, a nonprofit organization can operate with inclusive, democratic governance while preserving its mission by maintaining its charitable status.

  Disadvantages: Nonprofit organizations can sometimes have difficulty accessing resources while maintaining discretion over the use of those resources in implementing their mission. Creating a subsidiary corporation and then having that corporation raise capital is possible, but the nonprofit must be careful to navigate considerations of segregating governance and understand any implications from the activities or income generated by the for-profit subsidiary in order to not jeopardize its tax-exempt status (typically, this requires paying "unrelated business income tax," or UBIT). This often requires professional support, which can be costly and time consuming.

There is no one perfect legal entity for Next Economy enterprises and organizations. Almost any legal entity can be used or adapted to express Next Economy principles.

4

Personal Strategies and Life Design

W e cannot get to an economy that works for the benefit of all life without changing ourselves. What are the habits, behaviors, and norms that need to change on a collective level? What about you, as an individual? How do you design your life to better align with your vision for the Next Economy?

Next Economy Life Design

In many parts of the world, there are overarching systems and cultural norms that dictate "normal" pathways individuals tend to follow with regard to meeting the basic needs of living. For example, the "normal" U.S. pathway of getting a job to pay for your needs has been shaped by power, wealth accumulation, white supremacy, and colonization. This is different from historical and contemporary cultures where needs are met via gift economy or other forms of reciprocity. Life design offers an opportunity to counteract these oppressive histories and move towards economies that embrace a wide variety of ways to meet human needs.

The type of life design we are advocating seeks to question excessive consumption patterns because an economy that works for the benefit of all life is not possible without a significant overhaul of dominant culture. We have said many times in our MBA live sessions, "If every company were a B Corp, there would still be an existential crisis." This is because B Corps (and the broader corporate social responsibility movement) do not necessarily challenge the fundamental notion of how much to consume. Additionally, it is widely recognized that consumption levels in the affluent world, as well as large corporations, are largely responsible for the climate crisis, not to mention the human rights abuses associated with this level of consumption. Tragically, despite being the least responsible for this consumption, low-income communities and communities of color often bear the brunt of the impacts of climate change. We believe that humans are on track toward self-destruction through adverse outcomes of planetary resource depletion unless a dramatic transformation of consumption patterns occurs (especially in the Global North).

Life design asks you to rethink your complicity in the systems that force extraction and inevitably lead to suffering and harm. Life design is practiced not as a lone individual, but as a participant in a community of practice, a movement of people finding ways to support each other in this collective redesign process. If humanity can remember and reinstate a world where gift economy, trust, and cooperation are reclaimed, we can meet our needs via thoughtfully designed and trusting relationships between each other.

Figure 3 demonstrates three different pathways on the journey to rebalance your relationship with meeting your needs. The top line displays the polarization between production and consumption that constitutes much of the world today. Wealth often results in increasing distance from primary production, resulting in consumers who are dependent upon the nonaffluent populations who generally produce those goods and services. In life design, we are advocating for a move to the bottom line, towards more primary production and more trusting relationships between consumers and local producers. As you close the gap between consumption and production you can establish more satisfying, connected, and nonexploitative relationships with necessities such as food, fiber, shelter, energy, and water.

Many of you will find yourselves on the path of a highly dependent consumer. You may not have much of a relationship with those who produce most of the food and materials you consume. Healing this chasm can be a part of the transition to the Next Economy. We believe it is possible to move closer to a world of self-sufficient producers with deep knowledge of all that it took to provide access to food, clothing,

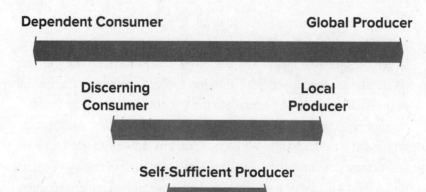

FIGURE 3: Consumer–Producer Pathways
Source: Lift Economy

water, and other forms of sustenance. Indeed, many Indigenous communities around the world offer lived experiences of thriving in balance with the means of production and consumption.

Another example of balancing production and consumption is agroecology. Agroecology, a type of sustainable farming that works with nature, constitutes a cornerstone for many global communities. Agroecology is a critical pathway of bioregional productivity that gives communities agency over some level of the production for their own sustenance—without compromising natural ecosystems. The more you strengthen your connection to the means of production, whether by heightening a sense of relationship with the producers you rely on or by attaining a level of self-sufficiency in your own ability as a producer, the more you are able to question dominant assumptions about how transactions must occur and reimagine new pathways for meeting societal needs.

Lastly, the decisions you make about how you design your life affect additional decisions you can (or cannot) make to interface more fully within the journey of transformation towards an economy that benefits all life. LIFT Partner Erin Axelrod, over the course of her decade with LIFT, has reduced the amount of money she has paid on rent, at times even to zero dollars, based on trust-based relationships and a rekindling of nonmonetary (which she calls "more-than-monetary") exchange. This has facilitated her ability to keep her salary relatively low, thus expanding her ability to work with clients, nonprofits, and other communities she seeks to serve regardless of their ability to pay. She has turned a life-design practice of keeping rents low into a vehicle for personal transformation and a mechanism for being able to give her gifts more fully to the world.

Hierarchy of Consumption

Most of this book focuses on each reader's potential role as an entrepreneur, intrapreneur, or leader at an organization. However, a component of the Next Economy transition depends on how you hold your role as consumer. For example, the organization Black Minimalists has a directory sharing stories of couples and individuals and communities who are liberating themselves from the traps of capitalism. These "traps" are mainstream narratives such as "in order to eat, you must buy food" or "in order to be housed, you must pay rent." Although these narratives have very real impacts on people's lives (and positionality and privilege play significant roles here), they are traps because they also act to squelch creativity. Humanity desperately needs new stories of what is possible if we are to survive as a species. Stories can show how to be free without exclusively relying upon financial wealth for acquiring and meeting our needs.

The hierarchy of consumption is a series of questions that help nudge you toward being a more empowered consumer. Note that each person will have their own constraints and opportunities based on privilege, positionality, and preference. When considering what to do about a particular good or service, ask yourself:

1. **Do I need it?** First determine if a good or service is truly needed or if the BAU economy is manufacturing the feeling of a need.

2. **Do I *really* need it?** Because of the BAU economy's insidious ability to convince people of manufactured needs, it is important to ask this question again with an open heart and mind.

3. **Can I borrow it?** Consider whether you need to own it or if access to it would suffice. Can you borrow it from libraries, neighborhood groups, friends, or buy-nothing clubs?

4. **Can I make it?** Perhaps you can learn a new skill and make it. One beauty of this kind of skill-building is that it creates opportunities for you to then pass this skill on, giving gifts to others, and showing up in a more contributive way in society.

5. **Can I get it used?** Can you find it at a thrift store? Rescue it from the trash? Can you organize a swap to harvest the plethora of goods lying dormant in many people's homes and closets?

6. **Can I get it from a local ethical producer?** This offers you the opportunity to form a relationship with someone and to invest in Next Economy ways of doing business.

7. **Can I get it from a reliable certifying body?** This represents the farthest distance from direct relationship (more middlemen) yet offers a stand-in for goods you cannot source directly from folks living in your bioregion.

Transaction Alternatives

Transaction alternatives include divesting, investing, bartering, gifting, sharing, using timebanks, and using alternative currencies. Transaction alternatives help you move away from the overreliance on money to meet your needs.

Divest

Divestment means reallocating money or human energy away from BAU practices—thus taking away power from the BAU economy. Many readers will recognize divestment as a potent tool that has been used to help end apartheid in South Africa, defund companies associated with the Dakota Access Pipeline (#DefundDAPL), and shift endowments out of fossil fuel investments.

Invest

Investment is the act of putting money, time, or other resources into something to gain a return or advantage. The Guild (theguild. community) is a worker-owned social enterprise whose mission is to build community wealth through community-owned real estate, entrepreneurship programs, and access to capital for Black and other communities of color. The Guild's Groundcover fund creates a pathway to ownership for Black and Brown people. The Guild raises the majority of its capital from larger institutions and investors. However, the Guild also offers legacy Black Atlanta residents and other community investors the opportunity to invest for as little as $100. This investment allows residents to own a portion of the financial benefit from development and reinvestment—which makes sense given these residents have built the cultural fabric of these neighborhoods in the first place.

Nwamaka Agbo, the CEO of Kataly Foundation and managing director of the Restorative Economies Fund, created the Restorative Economics framework to guide restorative investments. This method leverages (and invests in) the complementary aspects of community ownership and community governance to catalyze self-determination for political, cultural, and economic power.

In 2019, LIFT partnered with the Sustainable Economies Law Center (SELC) to launch the Next Egg, a project to support U.S. citizens in moving the $37 trillion of retirement savings currently locked up in traditional investments into community-based investments (you can read more about the harm these $37 trillion assets are doing in the *Harvard Law Review* article written by Jason Fernandes and Janelle Orsi in 2021).[25] The Next Egg's initial goal was to give people more control over how their retirement savings were invested—primarily via self-directed and worker-directed 401(k)s and IRAs. The theory was that this would unlock people's ability to invest in cooperatives, land trusts, and other enterprises that advance economic justice. However, as the Next Egg community tried to put these ideas into practice, it revealed some deeper problems—mostly centered around the Employee Retirement Income Security Act (ERISA) rules—that has led some at the Next Egg to change their approach. Visit thenextegg. org to join this ongoing conversation and learn more about the vision for reimagining and rethinking retirement in the United States.

Barter

Barter is an agreed-upon exchange of one good or service for another (as opposed to exchanging currency for both). It can be for housing, food, somatic coaching, therapy, bodywork, and more. There is a famous story of someone starting with a paperclip, and through a series of barter transactions, coming out at the end with a house. Barter often requires a deeper level of trust and rapport than financial exchange (although in the case of the paperclip to house, not necessarily). Barter, though not without its challenges, offers an alternative to relying exclusively on currency for meeting your needs.

Gift

Many people around the world meet their needs via the gift economy (conveying goods or services with no expectation of remuneration or reciprocity) and by being producers themselves (oftentimes by default). However, the world is trending away from this pattern. Once cultures that practice gift economy and mutual aid encounter the BAU economy (sometimes by dominance, war, colonialism, and conflict, and sometimes through the arrival of television), they are often severed from preexisting values of cooperation, care, and kindness. Reintegrating gift economy practices can help make progress towards a world that works for all life.

Share

Sharing provides access to resources freely without expectation of something in return. One of the ways it is distinguished from gifting is that ownership (in the case of goods) is not relinquished. In the past few decades, this concept of the "sharing economy" has been tragically co-opted for pursuit of financial gains by companies like Airbnb and Uber. Shareable, an online media platform, showcases stories, user manuals, and how-to guides around new and resurgent people-powered solutions paving a way forward based on sharing.

Timebanks/Alternative Currencies

A timebank is an alternative ledger system that records exchanges and values with each hour contributed as equal. The hour could be spent doing yard work, providing legal counsel, or cleaning someone's teeth. The late Edgar Cahn, often called "the father of timebanking," published copious literature on the benefits of having regional time-banks that support a vision of the world in which everyone is valued equitably. Alternatively, a credit-based currency system (sometimes called a local exchange trading system, or LETS) offers a nonfinancial platform for conducting transactions, but the value of each service or transaction is self-determined by the users rather than by hours. Skill-sharing platforms, like YING and Simbi, allow community members to trade their offerings (e.g., yoga lessons, guitar lessons, math homework assistance) without cash or other traditional financial transactions.

With all of the above choices, there are so many ways to align and attune your bank account, time, and energy to cultivate more meaning-ful ways to meet your needs and engage with your community. Now we'll look at some practices to help you implement some of these options.

Practices of Life Design

A key component for successfully practicing life design is to design around needs (shelter, food, joy, belonging, etc.) rather than around strategies (e.g., salary). A job or salary is only one strategy to meet your needs. By focusing on the need first, alternative strategies to meet your needs may present themselves—especially strategies that may not be readily apparent.

Another practice of life design is to consider three reference points you are seeking to emulate. These could be people whose life choices inspired you or communities thriving together to meet their needs. Studying, knowing about, and learning from reference points can help you avoid having to reinvent the wheel, and can also create a sense of mutuality and solidarity in a process that (in mainstream society) risks feeling overwhelming and isolating.

Once you have those reference points, we recommend that you broadcast your needs. If your friends, family, or even like-minded strangers do not know that you need something, how can they step up to support you? Often, a way to hold this is to reframe "asking for help" as "an opportunity for someone else to support you." Many people live their lives feeling isolated, and there is nothing that makes people feel more alive and their lives feel more meaningful than when helping someone. You can do this in many ways. You can call a friend and ask for specific support. You can attend a gathering and talk with folks at the gathering about your needs. You can email specific requests to communities or individuals who you think might be able to help you. It is highly likely that some people will be unable to help. This is fine and to be expected. For every person who says no, there are 20 more people willing to say yes. You just have to find them.

The myth of self-sufficiency is a trap that you can get stuck in when you practice life design. The dominant narrative can make you feel like the goal is to become an individual who has stepped outside the system. You may feel like you need to become free of reliance on money and completely self-sufficient in meeting your food, shelter, water, health-care, education, and purpose needs. This mythology is quite insidious and can negatively influence your subconscious.

Self-compassion and compassion for others are very important in this work. Acknowledge how hard this work is and how these life design practices are transforming centuries of colonization and oppression. Sarah Peyton, a neuroscience educator, says that not only is compassion a kinder path to take, but the science shows that kindness fosters more successful behavioral change. Meeting yourself with warmth and support is actually the more effective path of personal growth and transformation.

Case Study: Tiny Vignettes

When thinking of those individuals whose personal life designs inspire us, one consistent pattern is their ability to stay true to themselves. You are your own beautiful person. Your life design is going to look different from that others.

- Leah Penniman, who studied food systems and agroecology, was a new mom who found herself living in a food desert (a

(continued)

geographic area where residents have few to no convenient options for securing affordable and healthy foods—especially fresh fruits and vegetables). In asking herself the hierarchy of consumption question, "Can I make it?" (in her case, "Can I grow it?"), she and her partner founded Soul Fire Farm, which has since grown into one of the leading organizations combatting racism and food apartheid in the U.S. food system.

- Winona LaDuke, two-time vice presidential nominee, Harvard-trained economist, and executive director of Honor the Earth has committed a large percentage of her life energies in the "divest-ment" realm. Winona has mobilized people to rally for divesting public and private money from extractive fossil fuel corporations funding both the Keystone XL pipeline and Enbridge's Line 3—even getting arrested and putting her body on the line to stop construction. Her work does not stop there. Winona has spent a large amount of time investing her energy in building what she (and the Anishinaabe prophecies) calls "the Green path." The Green path is an economy rooted in Indigenous principles, regenerative crops (such as hemp), and cooperative economics.

- Ethan Hughes, founder of the Possibility Alliance in Belfast, Maine, is deeply committed to divesting from the BAU economic systems. The Possibility Alliance is designed to be a self-sustaining homestead, educational facility, and community attempting to function outside of capitalism while giving and receiving offerings of food, knowledge, and living space, all for free. The goal is to demonstrate a community design that is realizing the possibility of meeting everyone's needs.

5

Vision Alignment

Y ou have had an introduction to the Next Economy. You have learned about the principles of Next Economy organizations. You have learned about legal structures and life design. What if you wanted to start (or grow) an organization and express those principles? What are some keys to success? Where do organizations typically get tripped up and fail? In our experience, one of the biggest determinants of an organization's success or failure is whether or not they have an aligned vision for the impact they would like to create in the world.

Impact Vision

An impact vision is a vision for the positive social and environmental effects your organization aspires to create in the future. Having an impact vision for your organization (that everyone in your organization is in alignment with) is one of the single most critical factors for the success of your endeavor. Tragically, many organizations skip this step and assume a basic alignment. Each individual in the organization probably possesses a distinct vision for what the organization will be like in the future. Establishing and maintaining overlap or alignment of these separate visions is a fundamental investment that enables the organization to make clear, achievable (yet emergent) plans, work efficiently in the present, and greet new opportunities with ease and confidence. Your vision could be used in recruiting, orientation, culture building, stakeholder engagement, and marketing. Encourage it to live somewhere within the organizational culture where it can be frequently referenced. Morale can be enhanced by the sense of connection and purpose. And, depending on the goods or services provided, the market is likely to notice when team members are oriented around an aligned impact vision—potentially reducing costs in marketing, sales, and service.

One way to test for alignment is to share your vision of what the world would look like if your organization is successful in manifesting its intended social and environmental impact. You can then ask where the company is now in relation to that vision and how you plan to get there. If the vision and goals are clearly articulated, easy to access, and understood by your organization's key stakeholders (and they have been involved in creating them), then you have a firm foundation upon which to build a successful organization.

However, it is very rare that organizations have their visions articulated to this degree. A process of vision alignment that you can facilitate consists of three main steps:

Step 1: Collect individual responses. Have individuals in the organization share with each other a vision for the success of the organization. Examples of questions include:

- How would you describe your organization's impact on the world over the next one year, three years, and ten years?
- What are some examples of impact goals that you would like to see the company strive for?
- What makes working at this organization satisfying?
- What would you change or add to create a more satisfying and engaged work environment?
- What kinds of team and culture-building activities would you like to see the company try in the next couple of years?
- List any elements or features of your organization that you envision growing in the next one to three years.
- What is working well in your current business model?

- What is NOT working well in your current business model?
- What ideas do you have for company-wide goals for the following year?

Step 2: Conduct a pattern analysis. Find overlapping patterns in the individual visions and try to articulate an aligned vision. An objective third party can sometimes be helpful in the work of reading and distilling the patterns. Finding repeating themes of aligned elements from individual visions can be challenging because individuals often use different language to articulate their personal vision. Look for common language. Where possible, encourage personal visions to be as specific (and measurable) as possible. This makes it easier to find repeating themes but can constrain freedom of expression. Re-present patterns of alignment or repeating themes as "guesses" and facilitate discussion to clarify publicly what is in alignment and what might be a divergence.

Step 3: Seek alignment by working through divergences. Highlight where people's visions diverge and determine if there are possibilities for shifting or letting go of aspects of individual visions in order to achieve collective alignment. Through discussion, either reconcile the divergence or create space for public acknowledgment of the divergence. For example, support the individual holding the divergent element to "publicly grieve" or "let go" of that element as something that will not be part of the aligned vision for the organization. This public grievance process is related to Next Economy Principle 7: Embody Transparency. This does not mean that the individual needs to let go of that element for their personal life. However, it needs to be acknowledged that it will not be part of the aligned vision for the organization.

It is not uncommon to trigger stakeholder attrition in a vision alignment process. For example, someone might realize that the organization is not the right fit for them. That can be a very unsettling aspect of vision work—yet it is critically important. This realization could save an enormous amount of energy when conflict starts to result from a divergent vision. When you have only implicit (as opposed to explicit) alignment, people may start operating on their individual, divergent visions. This can produce subtle tension at first, but it can spiral into profound conflict that can break the organization apart.

In our experience, the most common areas of personal vision divergence from collective vision fall into the following categories. We encourage you to bring special attention to these areas during the alignment process.

- Money, income, and personal security strategies
- Growth, team, and scale of the organization
- Investors who come into an organization with a vision that is in conflict with your own

Cadence and Adaptation

Once you finish crafting your vision for the future, what are the chances it is 100 percent accurate? Not likely. This is why it is important to create a revisioning schedule. The cadence and adaptation of your schedule depends on the stage of development of your organization. One way to think about this work is to divide it into three stages of organizational development: feasibility, proof of concept, and scaling.

- *Feasibility:* A startup. An organization at this stage is determining whether their business model is viable.
- *Proof of concept:* An organization that has achieved some repeatable sales or transactions and demonstrated market traction. Even with some positive indicators, it is still unclear whether the company's business model can actually build a team and run a sustainable company.
- *Scaling:* An organization at this stage has stabilized and is able to generate sustainable income. The organization also has certain systems in place to help it grow, refine, and evolve.

You can see that the organizational design checklist in Figure 4 has stars to indicate which design tasks are most relevant to organizations at different stages of development. This is based on general trends we have seen from the hundreds of social enterprises with which we have worked. For example, if your organization is in the feasibility stage, spending time on your vision articulation is critical. But mapping out your succession strategy at an early stage (unless you choose a cooperative or

DESIGN			
VISION	**CULTURE**	**STRATEGY**	**OPERATIONS**
Vision Articulation *	Strategic Recruiting and Hiring Plan *	Market & Industry Research *	Operating Projection *
Vision Accountability & Revisioning **	Core Values **	Strategic Positioning *	Organization Structure *
Goal Setting **	Cultural Investments **	Messaging and Branding **	Accounting System *
Succession Strategy ***	Orientation and Training Plan ***	Marketing Plan **	Organization Rhythms **
	Performance Enhancement Plan ***	Sales Plan **	Reporting **
		Strategic Partnerships **	Policy and Procedure ***
		Decision-Making ***	Continuous Improvement ***
		Strategic Planning and Review ***	

KEY			
Stage of Development:	Feasibility *	Proof of Concept **	Scaling ***
Primary Focus:	*Business model seeking*	*Build your team and systems*	*Grow, refine, and evolve*
# of Project Areas:	7	10	7

FIGURE 4. Organizational Design Checklist
Source: Lift Economy

trust-owned structure that has succession and mission durability built in) would probably not have a large impact on your organization's ability to succeed. Similarly, an organization in the proof of concept phase would want to work on defining its core values before creating its performance enhancement plan.

Once the systems and tasks appropriate to your organization's stage of development are in process, you will want to work on crafting a revisioning schedule so that you can monitor how the company is doing. Notice that you may want to check in more frequently at earlier stages of development. For example, your feasibility-stage company might test a product or service, collect feedback from your customers, make improvements based on that feedback, and then pivot the company's offerings in a relatively small amount of time. In contrast, a 50-year-old scaling-stage company with a large staff and a well-established market is probably not going to radically pivot its service offerings every year. Scaling-stage companies often evolve more gradually.

The rhythms graphic in Figure 5 is designed to give you a basic framework and timeline for revisiting your design tasks. Please note that there is a different rhythm or cadence depending on your organization's stage of development. For example, earlier-stage companies often have quicker cycles for revisiting tasks. Later-stage companies often have more protracted cycles. Organizational rhythms are covered in more detail in the "Organizational Structure, Roles, and Tasks" section of "Part 8: Operational Systems."

ORGANIZATIONAL RHYTHMS			
ORG AREA	**TOPIC**	**TIME**	**DESCRIPTION**
Annual			
Vision	Vision Accountability	day long	How did the company perform on its strategic goals from last year?
Vision	Revisioning	day long	How is the company progressing on its vision? What, if any, adjustments need to be made to the vision?
Vision	Strategic Goal Setting	day long	What are the top 3–6 goals for the company for the next year?
Culture	Core Values	day long	Is the company behaving in alignment with its core values? Do they need to be changed?
Quarterly / Seasonal			
Strategy	Strategic Retreat	half day	
Monthly			
Culture	Cultural Investments	2–4 hrs	Company lunch, happy hour, sports team, field trip, etc.
Strategy	Board Meeting	2 hrs	
Operations	Org Team Meetings	90 min	
Accounting	Monthly Report	30 min	
Weekly			
Delivery	Production Meeting	1 hr	
Sales	Sales Pipeline	15 min	
Accounting	Cash Flow	15 min	
Daily			
Delivery	Stand up	5 min	Who is doing what today?

FIGURE 5. Organizational Rhythms
Source: Lift Economy

Goal Setting

Often, vision alignment discussions can be overly general. For example, if part of the vision is to "take care of people," you will probably get a lot of agreement. Who would not want to take care of people? As discussed earlier in the "Impact Vision" section, we encourage folks going through this process to keep the vision specific enough to identify subtle disagreements and misalignments with the vision. One way to seek out divergences is to use goals and hypotheticals.

For example, what might be an appropriate metric if your goal is to "create happy people in your community"? The metric might be attaining an average score of 90 percent or higher on a happiness survey that you administer to 1,000 folks in your community in December of the following year. In this example, something that could be generally agreed upon ("create happy people") is made very specific. The benefit of making something specific—even overly or falsely specific—is that it provides a forcing function to discover alignment or divergence.

Hypotheticals are similar. For example, pretend your team discusses a vision of "providing food to the local community." To dig for divergence or alignment with this vision, you might propose that you create a four-person team that works at least 20 hours a week and provides 3,000 meals to local community members every April. Your hypothetical might trigger a reaction in another team member. That person might say, "Wait a minute, I'm not sure if I want to be part of this organization if that is the vision we are holding." This reaction, while potentially unsettling, is not necessarily bad. Stakeholder attrition in this process can and will happen. Getting the right people onboard can save you from the enormous amount of conflict and friction that occurs from a collection of people working together without having done the work of checking for vision alignment.

There is an old saying in business: "Your strategic plan is outdated as soon as it is finished." Although this saying is not meant to be taken literally, there is truth to the underlying sentiment that everything changes. Given this, how do you account for goals that you have committed to but may want (or need) to change midyear? For example, what happens if your organization creates a specific goal to provide 3,000 meals to local community members every April and an opportunity arises to give back some of the land your organization owns to the local Indigenous people? How do you consider whether to transition your organization to the new opportunity for impact that has emerged? In this and other types of scenarios, you can go back to your impact vision and check the various opportunities that are available against the spirit of the vision. It is also important to remember that goals are directionally useful—they should not be rigid destinations that no longer feel authentic or do not take new developments into account.

Every organization should have their own goal-setting rhythms. Early-stage organizations might have them quarterly. More established organizations might have them annually. To increase the likelihood that you achieve (or make significant progress towards) your goals, make the goals accessible and visible to the team, and ensure that at least one person is accountable for any relevant milestones.

Example: Vision → Goals → Strategies → Tactics → Tasks

Most organizations (even large ones) are able to orient around no more than six to eight company-wide goals. It is not a good idea to have a large number of goals for the year. If everything is a priority, then it is much harder to be strategic with your time and energy. There can be a lot of strategies and tactics that flow from each goal. For example, let's assume you sell almond butter made from organic almonds grown with regenerative agricultural practices. One of your goals is to increase gross revenue by $100,000 by the end of 2025. A strategy to reach that goal could be to create a new product—an organic, fair trade chocolate almond butter. To test that strategy, a tactic could be to interview 10 prospective customers to see if they would be interested in chocolate almond butter. A different strategy to increase your revenue could be to start selling at local farmers' markets in the region. A tactic that flows from this strategy could be researching which of the local farmers' markets in your region get the largest number of shoppers.

- **Goal:** Increase revenue by $100,000 by end of 2025

  Strategy 1: Add a new chocolate almond butter flavor

  Tactic 1: Interview 10 prospective customers about their preferences

  - Task 1: Create a list of customers to interview
  - Task 2: Create a list of questions to ask
  - Task 3: Schedule calls with customers

  Tactic 2: Research what other almond butter companies are offering

  - Task 1: Identify five most similar almond butter companies
  - Task 2: See if any of the other almond butter companies would be willing to share their experiences about launching new flavors

  Strategy 2: Start selling at local farmer's markets in your region

  Tactic 1: Get a rough idea of the time, energy, and cost of selling at different farmer's markets

  - Task 1: Research how much each farmer's market charges vendors
  - Task 2: Reach out to different farmer's markets to see if they have open slots for new vendors

6

Culture

The next stop on the journey is taking a closer look at culture. If your team has a shared vision, but you lack a set of core values, cannot communicate with each other, and do not have an equitable, inclusive, and democratic culture, you are very unlikely to succeed. In this part of the book, we will explore the critical components of building a supportive, collaborative, and inspired culture that can sustain your team over the long term.

What Is Culture in the Next Economy?

If vision alignment is the "what" and "why" of your organization, culture is critical to answering "how" you will actually get there. We define *culture* as the shared sets of values, beliefs, behaviors, and investments that nourish and care for humans as they endeavor to create mutual benefit in the world. In many ways, what you are trying to do is to develop cooperative workplace values in a dominant society that rewards, promotes, and elevates a mindset of hyper-individualism. See Figure 6 for examples of different cultural worldviews.

Culture Happens by Default

When you have humans together, you have culture—whether you intentionally try to create a particular culture or not. It happens by default. Therefore, you want to create a safe, supportive, and

EXTREME COMPETITIVE CULTURE	SUSTAINABLE COOPERATIVE CULTURE	EXTREME COOPERATIVE CULTURE
Compete with others	Cooperate, including collaboration with allies	Cooperate within; collaborate only with others your group fully agrees with
Seek advantage and winning	Seek understanding and effective action	Seek attention as connection
Have skill? Use to dominate	Have skill? Teach with discernment	Have skill? Give away indiscriminately
Loudest voices win	Collaboration/consensus with discernment	Consensus with no discernment
I-oriented (individualistic, focus on self)	We-oriented (communal, focus on self in balance with others)	Us-oriented (hyper-communal, self subsumed to group
Independence encouraged/celebrated	Interdependence encouraged/celebrated	Codependence encouraged/celebrated
Dis-integrated	Integrated with differences valued	Individual needs/strengths lost
Capitalize on circumstances	Empathize with circumstances	Pity circumstances
Protect (resources and emotions, with no risk)	Share (resources and emotions, with boundaries)	Share (resources and emotions, without boundaries)
Make others responsible	Recognize personal and collective responsibility	Over-own personal responsibility
Differences threaten me	Differences are interesting	Differences threaten the group
Narcissism based on being "the best" and not needing to care	Not narcissistic; self is valued member of valued team	Narcissism based on emotional neediness met by group
System serves me	Service to others	Martyrdom

FIGURE 6. Comparing Cultural Worldviews and the Behaviors That Come from Them
Source: Lift Economy, adapted from Ma'ikwe Ludwig's *Together Resilient: Building Community in the Age of Climate Disruption*

motivating environment. If you do not, you will not be leveraging the full potential of your team. If you have a team that has committed to a vision of creating mutual benefit through the pursuit of a common vision, you need the team to commit to an equally aspirational culture to get there. If culture is not designed to be aspirational, it will be mediocre. Your team will have a keen sense of where the comfort of the whole group lies and there will be a natural tendency to cluster around this safe middle ground.

Creating an Aspirational Culture

If the individuals collectively opt into an aspirational culture and corresponding cultural investments, they are agreeing to hold themselves and each other accountable to a higher standard of behavior and performance. They will be committing to learning and improving together. This includes the brave practice of identifying mistakes and opportunities for improvement, harvesting the learnings from these moments, and designing the next steps forward based on the new information. This becomes a culture of continuous learning that taps into the intrinsic motivation of individuals to achieve mastery.

Green Canopy NODE, a vertically integrated construction technology firm and fund manager in Seattle, invests in their culture by having all staff participate in defining their core values annually. Each team member is then evaluated according to how they are expressing each value. This creates engagement and tangible reinforcement for the team to cocreate their aspirational culture.

Strengthening Community Glue

Organizations that make small investments sustained consistently over time (sometimes referred to as "community glue") can produce very positive results. Examples include a shared mindful moment prior to starting a meeting, a short personal check-in when meeting with teammates, and time at work devoted to workshops and team-building retreats. These can all create profound shifts in how teammates support themselves and each other in their shared journey.

World Centric, a compostable serviceware company, has Friday lunch-and-learn sessions where staff view a short presentation or video on a relevant social or environmental issue and then hold an open discussion. This invites staff to be actively engaged in their own education, critical thinking, and team dialogue.

Assigning Accountability

One risk in this process is that everyone agrees company culture is important, but no one is accountable for ensuring the culture is meeting your team's standards. Therefore, we recommend that your team assign someone to be a culture lead and someone else to a culture support role. For example, if your team chooses a core value of creativity, your culture lead can help plan a monthly cultural investment of making art, music, song, or dance together to activate that value.

CoLab Cooperative, an international technology developer, has a team member in charge of regular happiness check-ins with all members and supports them to solve problems and get support as needed. Activity from this role is presented in a regular report to the board of directors for accountability and team awareness.

Beware of Overcorrecting Your Culture

You should also be mindful of making an overcorrection when designing your company culture. For example, we have seen many groups react to the extremely competitive culture of the BAU economy by being extremely or overly cooperative. While this may be admirable, it can also be profoundly slow, inefficient, and frustrating. Yana Ludwig, in her book *Together Resilient: Building Community in the Age of Climate Disruption*, advocates for what she calls "sustainable cooperative culture," which seeks the middle path between extreme competitiveness and extreme cooperation.[26]

Values and Their Purpose

It is very difficult—if not impossible—for a company to create a healthy, dynamic, and supportive culture without having shared values. Values are a company's principles, standards of behavior, or judgment of what is important in order to achieve the company's vision. The process of naming the values, defining them together, and then bringing them alive in the organization is how you design and build culture. When values are aligned at an organization, employees are more engaged, growth and development is encouraged, decisions are easier to make, and teams have a stronger sense of mutual trust, support, and solidarity. When organizations lack values alignment, there is often conflict, tension, long meetings, and other dysfunctional aspects of culture that cost the organization time, money, and the potential for positive impact.

Defining Habits, Behaviors, and Norms

The specific words that companies choose for their core values are less important than collectively defining the habits, behaviors, and norms that are associated with the word. The habits and behaviors are what can be assessed, recognized, celebrated, and rewarded. For example, the word *integrity* could be chosen as a core value. What is meant by integrity? What kind of habits are associated with integrity? How does a team function as related to integrity? Words can mean very different things for different people. Some folks may feel that being on time for meetings is the highest manifestation of integrity. For others, it might mean what projects their team chooses to prioritize and pursue. If folks are consistently showing up five to ten minutes late to meetings, some may feel like their organization is acting out of alignment with its value of integrity. Others may strongly disagree. The behavior itself is not the issue. It depends on what the company has agreed to rely on. Doing the work to collectively define the habits, behaviors, and norms of what integrity looks like in practice will help reduce conflict and tension in the organization. The steps to do this in your organization are described in more detail later, in the "Breaking Down the Process" section.

Acknowledging and Celebrating Your Values

Once your values are consensual, your organization should aim to bring them alive by acknowledging them and celebrating them. One idea is to make space at the end of every team meeting to appreciate behaviors that demonstrate one of your core values. For example, "Thank you for jumping in and supporting me on the call yesterday. That is an expression of our value of solidarity. I'm so grateful that you brought that into the work we do together." Naming and celebrating the values again and again builds up your team's muscle. Pushing towards these aspirational ideas begins to transform your culture. Another example is a client of ours who finishes every week with "fails of the week." The vulnerability of this practice has helped employees better understand that failure is a way for them to learn. This has transformed their team's relationship to failure and has unlocked the team's potential for innovation and created more honesty in team communication.

Who Should Be Involved in Developing the Core Values?

Values can end up feeling stale and easily forgettable if the process of defining them is not thoughtful and inclusive. We discourage the CEO or other top leadership from developing the values and then dictating them to the rest of the company. The organization will be vulnerable to dysfunction and conflict unless the larger team has agency and engagement in the process. Having values that everyone has affirmed and agreed to will create a sense of common ground that can be useful in addressing tensions. Employees can reference the habits, behaviors, and norms to create a safer space to provide feedback and call people into difficult conversations.

Breaking Down the Process

Here is a process you can use to identify and align on your core values:

- **Step 1.** Have folks begin to list some of the words they would like included as a core value. If desired, you can use simple technology (like Google Forms) to capture some of the words. This can either be done real time or completed ahead of the values alignment exercise.

- **Step 2.** Once folks have input their suggestions, begin to look for patterns that you can cluster together. Clustering is not necessarily done strictly by dictionary definitions. It can be done based on the meaning of the word to the group (which may differ from the dictionary definition). Sometimes the definitions that emerge are novel and based on someone's interpretation of a word in a particular context.

- **Step 3.** Some people are very attached to certain words. The key is finding a workable pathway. An external facilitator can be helpful to listen to and encourage each person to define what a particular word means to them.

- **Step 4.** If there is attachment to a particular outcome or word choice, try to look for consensual alignment that works for most of the group.

- **Step 5.** It may be workable for folks to list sub-values within a core value. This allows you to have one word as your core value, but with multiple other words that form a constellation around it.

- **Step 6.** We recommend a target of roughly three (and no more than five) core values. This allows them to be memorable, referable, and tied to specific behaviors and norms.

- **Step 7.** Begin to write down the habits, behaviors, and norms tied to each value. This gives employees a navigational device to sense how the activities they (and the company) are doing on a day-to-day basis are connected with the values.

Case Study: Animikii Indigenous Technology
ANIMIKII.COM

Animikii is an Indigenous-owned digital agency and Certified B Corp. They work with leading Indigenous-focused organizations from all industries to drive positive change for Indigenous peoples through technology. Not only are they doing very important work, but they are also doing it in alignment with their beliefs and values. They believe that Indigenous people have always been technologists. They believe that technology is a societal equalizer, an economic driver, a path towards self-determination, and an example of sovereignty being exercised. Animikii's company values are rooted in Indigenous traditions and their business decision-making is guided by their values. The Seven Grandfather Teachings from Anishinaabe culture—Humility, Truth, Honesty, Wisdom, Respect, Courage, and Love—inform their relationships with clients, partners, employees, contractors, and other collaborators. Every year, each Animikii team member creates an "Authentic Accountability Agreement" where they have the opportunity to align individual and team goals with their values. From professional development and innovation projects to giving back and volunteer opportunities, each goal is led by one of their seven values.

(continued)

Compensation

Individual compensation is an important and tricky consideration in Next Economy enterprises. Almost everyone still has basic needs that are met through cash compensation. With staff needing to pay for rent, food, healthcare, etc., you need to pay adequate wages in order to keep your staff stable and satisfied in their vocations. We will cover some of the strategies we see Next Economy organizations testing to try to bridge the sometimes sizable gap between what people can earn and what they could get paid at a similar BAU job due to the price parity paradox (discussed in "Part 2: Principles of Next Economy Enterprises").

Focus on Total Compensation

One principle that we see organizations using is a focus on total compensation rather than the take-home salary alone. Total compensation means salary plus bonus, profit-sharing, and all benefits including the quality of the work experience. You can expand benefits beyond more traditional items like healthcare, paid time off, and a 401(k) retirement plan. You can include things like personal coaching and skill development, democratic engagement, ownership and governance rights, flexible work schedules, and the ability to change and evolve job descriptions. Optimized workplace benefits include preventative healthcare or wellness services, cultural investments that invite people to bring their whole selves to work, and time for critical self-reflection, coaching, and mentorship. Education and professional growth opportunities can be meaningful components of total compensation.

We are even beginning to see companies experiment with providing affordable housing. For example, The Internet Archive, a nonprofit organization based in San Francisco, found that its employees were spending as much as 60 percent of their income on housing. The Internet Archive did something unusual about this—the organization decided to purchase an apartment building in San Francisco where the employees could live. This created permanently affordable housing for their workers (and other nonprofit workers in the area).[27]

Money is only directly correlated with happiness up to a certain point. After that point, more money only increases satisfaction marginally. So what else matters? Research shows that autonomy, mastery, and purpose combined with active and meaningful relationships are some of the key drivers of happiness and longevity. Next Economy organizations can proactively embed these elements into their work culture, strategies, and operational systems. These can result in a comprehensive or holistic compensation package that outperforms a traditional financial-only compensation approach.

Transparency and Self-Set Salaries

When considering salary levels, formulaic approaches to calculating salaries can be helpful in navigating what can be tricky terrain. Having pay levels that are set for different roles and functions in the organization can help ground these conversations. Buffer, a social media publishing platform, famously publishes all their current staff's salaries on their public website for all to see (a common practice for many government institutions as well). This type of radical transparency is refreshing compared to the extreme secrecy that most companies reserve for their salary information.

One leading practice is for people to set their own salaries. Although this can be quite shocking at first consideration, the book *Reinventing Organizations* by Frederic Laloux points to many implementations that have been quite successful. "Won't people just pay themselves too much?!" is a knee-jerk response to this practice and is understandable as workers have rarely been asked how much they want to earn but rather are subject to prevailing wages in most industries.

Self-set salaries have guidelines for how they are set and approved. The process requires at least basic financial literacy of the organization's business model, stage of development, and financial capacity. There may be reference points available for what salary ranges are common for each role. There is often a salary committee or an advice process that is required to approve the self-set salary. Dennis Bakke, former CEO of the AES Corporation, described his company's experimentation with self-set salaries:

> The individuals who participated in this approach were changed by the process. They had a much better understanding of how compensation affected the overall economics of the organization. They learned the value of seeking advice when they had to balance competing interests. They put the interests of other stakeholders on a par with, or even ahead of, their own. The process pulled team members together, and helped some make the transition from workers to businesspeople. It made them "owners" of their business. For the first time, they understood what it meant to be stewards. This method of setting compensation was stressful, successful, and fun.[28]

Pay Equity

Pay equity practices are an important part of any discussion about compensation. Some Next Economy organizations are developing compensation policies designed to align with organizational values of equity and reparatory frameworks. Organizations like Harmonize, a holistic organizational development consultancy, help develop policies that enable organizations to disrupt patterns of power and dominance to prioritize Black, Indigenous, and people of color through an equitable compensation framework. Harmonize explains:

> All compensation decisions, even ones in "traditional" models, involve subjectivity. Subjectivity is inherent in determining things like job performance or growth. Even if job performance is tied to objective key results, the process of deciding what objective key results to value is a space of human subjective judgment. Importantly, often valuing "objective" factors imports inequities inherent in our economic system.

For example, consider a company that compensates employees based on the amount of sales of a business-to-business product. If one sales person is white and the other sales person is Black, the Black person will be impacted by racism during the course of selling in a way that the white person is not. This might result in different objective sales totals, but those totals have been influenced by racism. The presence of racism could result in the white person getting a higher salary even though it is based on a seemingly objective metric. The choice to use that objective metric is subjective because it is ignoring the fact the two people are doing acutely different jobs: one is selling to business while benefiting from the biases of a legacy of racism, the other is selling to businesses while overcoming the biases of a legacy of racism.[29]

Given this reality, Harmonize helps companies construct a process around compensation that seeks to take subjective and other factors into account in order to achieve pay equity.

Recruiting

You will never get great results without having the right people on your team. However, even if you know that intellectually, you may not follow recruiting practices that lead to high-quality hiring. For example, many hiring mistakes occur, not because you hired the wrong person, but because you did not have the right mix of candidates from the start. A lot of our thinking on recruiting and hiring has been influenced by The Management Center (TMC). TMC helps leaders working for social change build and run more equitable, sustainable, and results-driven organizations. One reason we like TMC is that they offer a wide variety of free resources on effective management that center racial justice at every step. Here are some of the recommendations from TMC and our work at LIFT for different stages of the recruitment process:

- **Figure out the role/job responsibilities.** Do not start by writing a job description (that will come in due time). First, try to think of specific activities the person might be doing if they were in the role today. For example, "evaluate website analytics to identify trends and patterns," "seek earned media articles that grow awareness of our work," and "manage the development of creative for social campaigns and general reach building campaigns."

- **Get clear on the skills and knowledge the role requires.** What type of person would thrive in the work you identified above? What skills, knowledge, and general qualities should they have?

- **Identify your "must-haves" and "nice-to-haves."** Your must-haves are skills and qualities on which you will not compromise. Your nice-to-haves are skills and qualities that are a plus, but not a requirement. Having clear must-haves is important because it can reduce the natural tendency to give importance to things that are not indicative of how well someone will perform (e.g., style of dress, hairstyle, accent, appearance). Try to distinguish between qualities that tend to be inherent (e.g., self-awareness and emotional intelligence, attention to detail, compassionate communication, resourcefulness) and skills that can be more easily taught (e.g., familiarity with Salesforce, experience cold-calling, knowledge of supply chain logistics). Over time, inherent traits and qualities are much more likely to differentiate high performers than specific skills or knowledge.

- **Create your job description.** Your job description should explain the job responsibilities, list the qualifications you are looking for, and describe your organization. It can also be helpful to include a narrative description of what a typical day might be like in the role. This helps bring a dry list of bullet points to life and make it more real for candidates to imagine themselves in the role. A simple pie chart showing the rough time breakdown to be spent on the major task areas can help convey the role visually.

- **Think carefully about what materials you ask applicants to submit.** If you only ask for a résumé and cover letter, you may get a flood of applications. It can help narrow down your pool to request that applicants answer a number of questions before submitting their application. For example, Justice Funders, a worker self-directed nonprofit that supports transformation in philanthropy towards a Just Transition (i.e., building economic and political power to shift from an extractive economy to a regenerative economy) asks anyone applying for an open position to answer two questions:

1. How would you apply the Just Transition Framework in this role?
2. How would you practice Shared Leadership, Psychological Safety, and Emotional Intelligence with fellow team members?

Building a Qualified Pool of Candidates

Once you have figured out what you are looking for and completed a job description, how do you recruit candidates? Building your pool of qualified candidates is one of the most important factors in whether you hire the right person for the role. Refrain from posting your job openings publicly until you have tried direct outreach first. The goal is to get a small number of highly qualified candidates, instead of a large number of unqualified folks.

Potential Candidates

Think of your own network. Do you know anyone, even working somewhere else, who would be a good fit for this role? Write down all the names you can think of. Rather than emailing a job description to someone and asking if they are interested, try to set up a phone call or in-person meeting. This personal touch is often much more successful in gaining someone's attention. If you do not have a diverse network, reach out to others who do by finding sources who might be more likely to know Black, Indigenous, and other people of color; recent immigrants; LGBTQIA+ folks; people with disabilities; and more.

Connectors

Think of connectors—people who are not right for the job themselves but might know others who are. Go through your list of contacts to identify people who are connected to your organization or are acquaintances who might be good sources. Ensure you are reaching out to connectors that have relationships with traditionally marginalized communities. Again, try to speak with connectors directly by phone, video call, or in person. You will be surprised at how many more names you get when you spend a few minutes on the phone in conversation.

Public Postings

The most common—yet least effective—means of building a pool of candidates is posting your job opening publicly. If you do decide to post your job publicly, consider posting it to a small, targeted group first. For example, share the job in your newsletter or with specific groups committed to antiracism, social entrepreneurship, and climate justice. Try to avoid larger, generic sites like Craigslist and Idealist that can flood your inbox with unqualified candidates.

Building networks of personal and professional relationships—especially those that span racial, ethnic, gender, and other identities—are lifelong endeavors that need to be continually nurtured over time. Instead of reaching out when a new hire is needed, think of a process of continually networking and providing mutually beneficial value over the long term.

Accommodations

Different prospective applicants will have different abilities to apply to your position. Create accommodations for those who need it to help expand the pool of applications you receive. For example, allow people to answer questions from your application via audio or video. Many roles do not require formal writing skills. Do not make writing ability a barrier to applying—especially if it is not core to the position.

Interviewing and Selection

Once you have a pool of applicants, now your work begins to select the best candidate for the current position. The selection process typically consists of narrowing down the applicant pool at various stages of the process. The steps you take will depend on the position for which you are hiring, the organization's stage of growth, and the size and quality of your list of applicants. Let's examine some of the key steps.

Application Screening

As applications begin coming in, you will know right away (based on your must-haves) that some folks are not a great fit for the job. You can cross those folks off your list immediately. For others, it will take reviewing the materials more closely. Remember, your primary goal is to look for evidence of the must-have qualities you want for this role. In addition, try to be aware of three common types of biases in candidate evaluation:

- *Like me:* Humans tend to gravitate toward those whom they are most like—people who look, think, and feel similarly.

- *I like you:* You may like someone without knowing why. Liking someone and them being the right person for your role are two different things.

- *Dominant culture:* White, male, cisgender, heterosexual, Christian, affluent, able-bodied, and so forth; activist and poet Audre Lorde referred to this white male archetype as the "mythical norm" in which "the trappings of power reside within society."[30] Applicants who align to this mythical norm are often preferred.

The Management Center recommends using a hiring rubric in order to help mitigate bias in your hiring process.

Phone Screening

The second stage we recommend is a brief (20–30 minutes) phone call or video call with the top applicants. The goal of the phone screening is to ensure vision and values alignment. At this stage, you are not getting into the technical requirements of the job quite yet. Vision and values misalignment is one of the biggest (if not *the* biggest) reasons Next Economy companies fail. This call is also a time for the applicant to ask any clarifying questions about your organization and the role itself. If team capacity is stretched, there may be one person who does all the screening calls and then has one or more team members join subsequent interviews.

Interview Stage

The next stage is to set up a formal interview focusing on your must-haves. The goal at this stage is to find out how candidates have acted in the past (or to observe how they act in the present) to best predict how they will act in the future. To do this, here are some sample interview questions to probe for prior experience:

- *Tell me about a time you came up with a new approach for tackling a problem. What did you do? What was the result?*

- *Tell us about a time when you worked to make sure your workplace/team/project was a place where everyone—particularly those who identify as Black, Indigenous, and/or People of Color (BIPOC)—could participate and thrive. What was the situation and what was your contribution?*

- *Tell me about a time when you had a tight deadline. What was the project? How did you get everything done? How did you engage with others to ensure a diversity of perspectives?*

- *Tell us about a time you worked to address someone's concern and you weren't able to. What happened and what did you try? Were there lines of difference or power that made this tricky? What might you do differently next time?*

Job Simulation/Working Interview

It can be very helpful to your process to have candidates perform activities similar to what they would be doing on the job. The job simulation does not have to be separate from the earlier interview stage (or even the application or phone screening stages). Another option is to hire candidates for a more in-depth working interview. These are typically structured as between a half day and two weeks. Working interviews are paid and give a chance for the candidate and staff to directly work together on the actual tasks of the job. For example, one of our clients is an ecological design and landscaping company that does working interviews with all their applicants for field crew positions. These positions require very little formal writing or spoken interview skills. They do require coordinated teamwork, hard labor, and hands-on knowledge and experience with plants and tools. None of those "must-haves" come through on paper or in a seated interview but are well identified when working in the field with the rest of the crew.

Reference Checks

Do not skip this step. List the must-haves for the position you are filling. Cross off the qualities you are convinced the candidate has demonstrated during interviews and application exercises. Focus your reference checks on the remaining must-haves. Most people only give references who will speak highly of them. You may consider doing some of your own research as well. If you know people in the candidate's circle, reach out and ask them to give candid feedback.

Making Your Decision

Once you have gone through these stages, it is time to make your decision. Try to assess the candidates against the criteria you established at the beginning of this process. In addition, listen to your gut by asking yourself if you would be thrilled if this person came to work for you. You should also listen to the opinions of others who have been involved in the hiring process. Consensus by the group of people involved in recruiting, screening, and interviewing is a best practice. If more than one person voices concerns, take those concerns seriously.

No matter what, do not fill a vacancy with someone you think might not be the right fit. It does not matter how desperately you need to fill a vacancy. You will almost always be better off keeping the position open and searching for short-term solutions. You can delay the launch of certain projects. You can triage by shifting high-priority responsibilities among existing staff members. Over the long term, you will spend far more time and energy dealing with a bad hire than you will save by filling a vacancy with the wrong person.

Orientation

Now that you have found your new teammates, you can move into the process of onboarding or orienting them to your company and team. Here is some advice for ensuring your new staff member's first few weeks are a success.

Prepare in Advance

The last thing you want is to be unprepared for your new employee's start date. This can send unintentional messages about your workplace culture and expectations from the start. Create a checklist of the tasks you need to complete in order to effectively onboard your new hire. This checklist can include an initial training agenda that lays out everything you will want to cover with them. For example, for office workers, you should ensure that your team member's email, phone, computer, list of online accounts and passwords, and workstation are already set up before their first day.

Make New Employees Feel Welcome

On day one, you want your new employees to feel welcome, appreciated, and set up for success. This is a great time to review your company's vision, mission, and values (and the habits, behaviors, and norms that demonstrate those values). This focus upfront communicates the importance of the larger impact vision your organization holds. It is also a good time to review the employee handbook, existing workflows, and policies. One team we know would spend the entire first day orienting a new employee. They would meet the staff, tour the facility, and review the entire employee handbook page by page. It wasn't until the second day they would actually begin working on their job. Running such a strong day-one program helped create a deep sense of purpose and connection. This company had low turnover compared to rivals in the same industry, probably due in part to the care it put into its onboarding processes.

We also recommend that you do something special, such as a team lunch or happy hour—for your new staff members. Alternatively, if you are working remotely, consider offering new staff a care package (with homemade treats and other goodies) that arrives before their first day of work.

Align on Expectations

Alignment of expectations is one of the single biggest factors in the long-term success of your new hire. Knowing what is expected of them, how frequently they will be evaluated, and what success looks like is essential to cultivating their sense of belonging. We recommend creating explicit 30-, 60-, and 90-day goals for your new hire. This will help you and your new staff member align on essential activities for the first three months.

Check In Regularly

In the first few weeks, you may want to do shorter check-ins daily or every other day. After the first two weeks, switch to weekly. In the first month, you will spend a lot of time answering questions, sharing context, and debriefing. What are they finding most challenging? What sort of help might they need?

Performance Enhancement

"Performance enhancement" is a reframe of what most organizations call "performance evaluations." We have reframed it to emphasize the result that we want to achieve from the process. This points to the shift we want to make away from the traditional viewpoint of squeezing maximum value from a resource to supporting your staff to achieve personal fulfillment (while simultaneously supporting the needs of the organization).

Example Process

At LIFT Economy, our annual performance enhancement process asks team members to fill out self-reviews first. We then have a peer and/or manager complete the form. The different sections on the form include:

- **Core Values.** How well did I embody my organization's core values?

- **Key Cultural Habits and Behaviors.** How well did I demonstrate the specific habits, behaviors, and norms that are indicative of the core values?

- **Key Functional Tasks.** *(defined first by the reviewee and then added to by subsequent reviewers)* To what extent did I make progress towards and/or complete the specific tasks to which I was accountable during the evaluation period?

- **Custom Self Skill Assessment: Strengths.** *(created by the reviewee)* What were my areas of strength during the performance period?

- **Custom Self Skill Assessment: Areas of Growth.** *(created by the reviewee)* What were my biggest areas of weakness during the performance period?

- **Summary.** *(created by the reviewee)* Moving forward, what are the top three changes I could make to improve my performance and benefit the organization?

- **Summary.** *(created by peer/manager in review of the completed form)* Were there any major discrepancies and/or differences in the team member's self-evaluation and the evaluation provided by others?

- **Performance Excellence Plan.** *(created first by the reviewee, adjusted via feedback and support from the rest of the team)* What is my plan to implement the top three changes I identified earlier? What metrics and indicators will I use to measure my success?

Other organizations we work with also include input from others whom the staff member regularly interacts with (peers, vendors, partners, clients, etc.). These companies compile the feedback, analyze it for themes, and review it with the individual in order to cocreate their next set of future goals. Many people have never experienced this type of constructive feedback and support. It can result in inspired performance when done well.

Things to Avoid

- **Skipping and Constant Rescheduling.** Skipping and/or continually pushing back the performance enhancement process due to other projects may make staff doubt if their development is a priority for you.

- **Avoiding Difficult Conversations.** Don't avoid addressing tensions now and wait for a review that may be far away. This feeds into a culture of avoidance and acceptance of underperforming. Ideally, nothing in a performance evaluation should be a surprise, because you have been giving feedback throughout the year.

- **Assuming Poor Performance Is Only the Individual's Fault.** Many teams make the mistake of focusing just on an individual's performance. It could be the environment in which they are located. Instead, look at their team (or the whole organization) for insight into how you can all work better together. This can sometimes look like restructuring their role to better suit them and the organization overall.

Ideally, the previous sections have given you some insight into how Next Economy organizations approach hiring, retaining, and developing employees. The following sections go into facilitation and communication—two important skills that need to be cultivated within your organizational culture.

Facilitation

The ability to facilitate is an underrated and underappreciated skill. The speed and effectiveness with which humanity can bring about the Next Economy is connected to how skillfully groups of people can be moved towards a common goal. Successful facilitation is a prerequisite for organizations interested in Next Economy Principle 3: Democratize Governance. The contrast between good and bad facilitation is clear. In a poorly facilitated gathering, folks can feel excluded, angry, discouraged, and exhausted. In a well-facilitated meeting, participants can leave invigorated, refreshed, and with a clear sense of purpose. Good meetings help build resilient and effective movements.

What Is Skillful Facilitation?

Skillful facilitation entails more than just setting an agenda beforehand, doing check-ins, and moving through the content. Facilitation, when done effectively, helps ensure that the entire group is empowered, rather than a small subset of participants. This means that the facilitator should seek to ensure that all attendees get to participate and share ideas—not only those that feel most comfortable doing so.

Be Aware of Power Dynamics

Facilitators need to be aware of power dynamics and how they often marginalize folks of color, women, LGBTQIA folks, people with disabilities, immigrants, people who are not native speakers of the language, folks who have different levels of access to resources, and more. Effective facilitators are aware of how these dynamics show up in groups—and have strategies to mitigate and interrupt them. In addition, facilitators attempt to keep the group conversations on topic (and on time) in order to help move the group forward. Being able to understand and navigate these tensions will help make the meetings you lead more effective and more inclusive.

Case Study: Anti-Oppression Resource and Training Alliance AORTA.COOP

AORTA is "a worker-owned cooperative of facilitators and strategists devoted to helping our movements renew a stronger sense of liberatory vision, values, and purpose." AORTA's team is composed of highly regarded facilitation experts. The following information is from a resource AORTA created entitled "Tips on Naming, Intervening, and Addressing Systemic Power":

- Even organizations with great meeting processes inadvertently perpetuate barriers to full participation and access to democratic process.

(continued)

- Name it when it's happening.
  - "I'm noticing..."
  - "that I haven't heard from many people of color recently."
  - "that there's a lot of interrupting happening, and that it's happening along gender lines. I want us all to work to become more aware of that and change it."
- Refrain from saying things that people hear as name-calling.
- Ask questions to support self-inquiry.
  - "What makes you say that?"
  - "Can you tell me more about that?"
- Support the leadership of marginalized voices.
  - Allow people to respond on their own behalf.
  - Synthesize. "What I heard from this person is..."
- Create space for those you are not hearing from.
  - "I'm going to take a moment to see if anyone who hasn't spoken in a while has something to say."
  - "We've been hearing from a lot of men. Let's take a moment to see if any of the women, genderqueer, or trans folks in the room have something to say."

Example Process

Here is one way to structure and facilitate meetings, based on how our meetings are structured at LIFT Economy. There are also some general tips included below that can improve the quality of your meetings:

- **Preparation/Check In**
  - Choose a facilitator and a note taker. At LIFT, we rotate who facilitates and who takes notes so folks can build their skills and experience with each.
  - Mindful moment. Start the meeting with a mindful moment and/or a welcoming into the space.

– Check in. We often ask questions like "What is most on your mind right now?," "What is one thing you liked and one thing you did not like that happened this week?," or "What are you most excited about?" These short check-ins allow participants to feel more grounded and present for the meeting.

- **Set the Agenda**

Once people have been welcomed in, roles are set, and everyone has had a moment to ground themselves, it is time to set the agenda. We developed the meeting agenda template (Figure 7) to help create more efficient and inclusive meetings (a link to an editable copy of this template that you can use for your organization can be found at lifteconomy.com/mbabook). Here is an explanation of each of the elements of our spreadsheet:

– *Team Member Priority Vote:* Deciding which agenda items to discuss at a particular meeting has been one of the challenges we had at LIFT. We created a simple voting system that allows each team member to rank different agenda items. This helps ensure everyone's voice is heard. We allow agenda items to be added before a meeting and at the start. We also leave space at the beginning of a meeting for people to vote or for folks to propose any amendments to existing items. Whichever items have the highest average ranking are the ones we will prioritize first.

\multicolumn{14}{l}{TEAM MEMBER PRIORITY VOTE (1 = HIGH, 5 = LOW, NP = NO PREFERENCE)}
SB	KB	RH	EA	PS	AVE	Quorum	Type	Min	Lead	Topic	Description (add data if timely)	Link	Origin Date	Result
1	3	5	2	1	2.4	All	Discussion	15	PS	LIFT Team Retreat	Have we planned our annual retreat dates for 2023?		5/14/23	
3	4	2	3	2	2.8	All	Decision	25	RH	Marketing Hire	Proposal to move forward with posting marketing job description		5/28/23	
					0.0									
					0.0									
					0.0									

FIGURE 7. Meeting Agenda Template
Source: Lift Economy

- *Quorum:* How many people need to be present in order to discuss the topic. The choices are "all," "majority," or "some/any."
- *Type:* What is the purpose of this agenda item? Is it sharing information? Is it to try to brainstorm and generate ideas for solving a problem? Is it for coworking on something together? Is it to come to a decision? Being clear on the intention of the agenda item is very important.
- *Minutes:* How long the agenda item is anticipated to take
- *Lead:* The person taking the lead on framing the agenda item to the group
- *Topic/Description:* Name and brief description of the item
- *Link:* Any links to background information or other material
- *Origin Date:* When the item was first proposed, in order to track how long something has been on the agenda
- *Result:* What resulted from the agenda item? Options include complete, incomplete, moved to a separate meeting, and pending.

A best practice would be to have agenda items and details (topic, description, links, etc.) filled out ahead of time and circulated so that people could come prepared for the meeting.

- **Move through the Agenda**
  - Keep on topic and on time. Once your agenda is set, try to keep the meeting flowing in a direction that is beneficial for the group as a whole. Keep an ongoing list to write down ideas, questions, and topics for future meetings. This will help capture items that might otherwise have derailed the current agenda.
  - Ensure all voices are heard. LIFT has a practice that we call "going around the circle." This means that we allow every LIFT team member to give their thoughts on a particular topic, proposal, or decision before other members are allowed to jump in, debate, or comment. This helps ensure that the loudest or most privileged folks do not dominate the conversation. There

are many names for this ("talking stick," "go-around," etc.). People can always pass if they like. A signal of a healthy culture is when passing is normalized and frequent.

- Synthesize. When needed, try to synthesize what you are hearing participants say, especially emotions and values. This can help reassure folks that they are being heard, can help prevent miscommunications, and can build empathy and connection.

- Guide discussions towards decisions. One of the problems with meetings is that they can become a series of disconnected monologues that seem to go on forever. One cut-through we have found is to encourage folks to use the phrase "I propose that . . ." The purpose of this phrase is to narrow down a conversation to a specific next action. This can be very helpful in moving the meeting forward for the benefit of the group.

- **Next Steps**
  - Confirm key decisions. Ask if someone would like to take on the task (or assign someone to it). Try to identify a timeline and/or deadline to ensure there is accountability to the group.

- **Check-Outs**
  - Gratitude/Appreciation. At LIFT, we try to take a few minutes at the end of every team meeting to appreciate behaviors that demonstrate one of our core values. For example, "Thank you for bringing up the conversation about pay equity. This is a great example of our shared value of collective liberation."

- **Follow-Ups**
  - Share notes/recordings/action items. If a team member cannot make one of our meetings, we have an agreement to record the meeting and share it with that team member. That person then has one week to review the recording and get back to the team with any questions, comments, or concerns. This allows our team to remain flexible when life situations arise and we have to miss a meeting.

Communication

We have discussed vision and values and why they are the corner-stone, or critical success factor, of why organizations succeed or fail. Communication is directly tied to the organization's ability to act on its vision and values. And yet, effective communication is often marginalized as a focus area for many businesses. There are hidden costs to not investing in communication training for your organization. These costs include interpersonal stress, conflict, inefficiency, and staff turnover. We have also seen the cost be as high as the collapse of the entire organization.

Best Practices for High-Quality Communication

Unfortunately, there is no single recipe or script folks can follow that will always result in better communication. Context is very important. People have different experiences and will have different reactions. However, there are certain principles and practices that can lead to higher-quality communication. Here are some of the patterns we have identified:

- *Empathy:* Being sensitive to how each person brings their unique skills, lived experience, identities, background, and preferences to each meeting or interaction can dramatically enhance communication and connection.

- *Listening:* Active listening is the pathway of empathy. When someone else is talking, are you deeply listening to them, or are you trying to plan what to say next? Try to cultivate a practice of listening. Truly hearing someone can change or transform the most difficult circumstance. Nonviolent Communication (described later in this section) is a great practice to become a better listener and communicator.

- *Emotional intelligence:* Feelings are oftentimes more important than facts. If you are going around in circles in dialogue with someone, ask yourself what feelings may be underneath the surface of the conversation that need to be named.

- *Curiosity and openness:* Judgment can interrupt empathy, shut people down, inflame defensiveness, and reduce participation. Being open and authentically curious can greatly increase the chances of connection.

- ***Body language and tone:***
  - Your body language and your tone of voice can put people at ease, build trust, and draw others towards you. Or they can offend, confuse, and undermine what you are trying to convey. Being conscious of both is a continual practice.

- ***Medium of communication:***
  - Make sure you are using the right medium for the type of conversation you are having. Is a text message the right way to get my point across? Does an email really communicate my tone of voice? Should this be done in person? The benefits of pausing and reflecting on these questions can be very profound.

Introduction to Nonviolent Communication (NVC)

One of the best tools we have seen to enhance how folks speak and relate to one another is nonviolent communication. The philosophy of NVC states that a quality of connection is required in order to have the best chance of meeting everyone's needs. Part of NVC's model focuses on four components and how they can help establish a quality of connection.

1. *Observation:* Seek to observe a situation or action without evaluation or judgment.

2. *Feeling:* Understand that people experience varying emotions and physical sensations in each particular moment.

3. *Need:* Understand that you, as well as everyone else in the world, have needs and values that sustain and enrich you. When those needs are met, you experience positive feelings, and when they are not, you experience negative feelings.

4. *Request:* Learn to request clear and concrete actions that can be carried out in the present moment. You can begin to find ways to cooperatively and creatively ensure that everyone's needs are met.

NVC is helpful in that it distinguishes between needs and strategies. Needs are universally shared things such as connection, physical wellbeing, honesty, peace, meaning, play, and autonomy. Strategies are attempts to meet needs and are tied to particular people, places, or things. For example, owning a high-end sports car is not a need, it is a strategy—perhaps to seek connection, acceptance, find peace, create meaning, or strive for autonomy. This insight can help identify the needs behind harmful, unsafe, or overindulgent strategies. In NVC, shared needs are the gateway to empathy. Empathy is the pathway to a quality of connection. As was mentioned previously, a quality of connection is required in order to meet everyone's needs. This allows you to find strategies that work for everyone.

7

Strategy

S trategy is a carefully developed plan for running an enterprise in order to achieve one or more goals. Your strategy allows you to bring your products or services to market. It is important to understand how to do market and industry research, position your offering, and communicate your core value proposition. In addition, raising money from investors and accessing resources from your community should be done very thoughtfully. Your strategy should include understanding finance, the order of operations for seeking finance, available security structure options, and how to find the right investors. Finally, this section explores decision-making, governance, and creating strategic partnerships.

Industry Research:
Needs vs. Known Needs

One framework that is important to understand is the difference between "needs" and "known needs." Many ethically oriented people who are passionate about building the Next Economy see an enormous amount of need in the world. For example, you might firmly believe that your community would benefit from having access to healthy, nutritious, organic, regeneratively grown food. For you, this is a clear need. The question is whether it is a *known* need in your community.

Similarly, you might believe that the world needs mindfulness and meditation practices. Does the community you are trying to serve agree that this is a need? It is often a significant effort to bring a product or service to market and, unfortunately, we have seen many entrepreneurs put forth this effort without taking the time to validate that what they are trying to provide matches known needs.

Education-Based Selling

What happens when your product or service does not necessarily match the known needs of your target market? In this scenario, your enterprise might need to provide educational services to facilitate learning for members of your target market about certain issues that may be unknown to them. It can be difficult, challenging, and humbling to attempt to shift the awareness of something from a need to a known need. It may also be quite different from the thing that you originally wanted to do.

A good case study to highlight this concept is the company Seedles. Seedles was originally started to provide seed balls to urban farmers to help them grow cover crops. Seed balls are a beautiful technology popularized by Masanobu Fukuoka in Japan. The technique is to take compost, clay, and seeds and roll them into balls that you can deposit around the garden. Birds are unable to get the seeds. When the rains come you have a reliable cover crop. Seedles was spending a lot of time, energy, and money to sell the product, but it was not working. One day, a prospective customer came to them and asked if they could have 100 seed balls as an eco-friendly party favor for their kid's birthday. The customer also asked if they could add color to the balls. The folks at Seedles said yes and started using plant dyes to color the products. This completely changed their business model to wildflowers and habitat restoration for bees. Seedles are now one of the most popular eco-friendly Easter gifts. They had to grow very quickly because the demand for their products started to outstrip their supply. The key was finding the positioning that worked for the market.

Build, Measure, Learn

One framework that we would like to reference (with some hesitation, due to its widespread use in the BAU economy) is the Lean Startup methodology. Lean Startup, which is used in many traditional corporations and especially in the technology industry, was born out of the idea of the importance of building, measuring, and learning. Even though we do not fully advocate for Lean Startup (again, due to its association with the BAU economy), there is an element of simplicity and brilliance to the model that is worth exploring. In the Lean Startup methodology, the first step is to test your hypothesis as cheaply and easily as possible. This is called building a minimum viable product (MVP). In the case of Seedles, the hypothesis was that people need seed balls to provide cover crops for urban agriculture. The MVP for Seedles was to build a limited amount of their product and start trying to sell it. The second step is to measure the results. Are people buying your product? Are they expressing satisfaction? The last step is to make changes and build a new hypothesis. The folks at Seedles wondered if other parents might be interested in buying seed balls for their kids. They used plant dyes on all their products. They put up a new landing page on their website. They contacted parenting groups and offered their products for trial. This was part of a new build, measure, and learn cycle.

The System Is the Key

You need a system for capturing feedback about what is working and what is not working. It is critical to have numbers or metrics to better understand what is going on within the market or community you are serving. When we work with clients, we want them to know how well their positioning (a concept described in the next section) is working. We hope to see some metrics that show that their positioning is resonating with customers or that they have been adapting their products and services based on customer feedback. We get concerned when there is a gap between an entrepreneur's belief about what is needed in the world and what the market is willing to support.

Marketing and Positioning

One concept often used in the BAU economy is "segmenting, targeting, and positioning." Even though it is practiced in the BAU economy, Next Economy companies can still learn from this approach and apply the insights to help achieve their long-term impact vision. *Segmenting* is the process of dividing a broad population into subgroups according to certain shared factors. These groups may have common demographics (age, gender, etc.), geographic location, attitudes, behaviors, or a combination of similar characteristics. People may also belong to multiple market segments. For instance, a woman may be from Generation X (gender and age demographic), living in an urban area (geographic location), who likes to buy her food within walking distance (purchasing habit) from cooperatives or other socially responsible companies (attitude). *Targeting* refers to picking the market segments to which you would like to offer your goods or services.

The Venn diagram in Figure 8 shows the basics of strategic *positioning.* Your ideal strategic position is the central area where these three circles converge. You want to know yourself, the industry, and your market as well as possible.

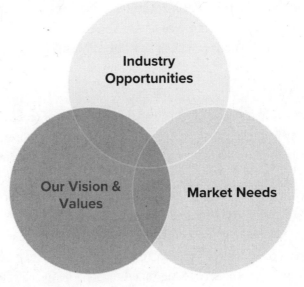

FIGURE 8. Strategic Positioning Venn Diagram
Source: Lift Economy

- *Your Vision and Values:* As an organization, what is your purpose? What are you trying to do in the world?
- *Industry Opportunities:* Who else is in your industry? Who else is offering similar products or services?
- *Market Needs:* Who is your customer base? What do they want?

It will likely take a number (perhaps even a large number) of build, measure, and learn cycles to help you refine your strategic position. That is OK. The following sections (along with the companion workbook) will help you continue to think about how you can get closer to the center of the Venn diagram.

Case Study: WholeTrees   WHOLETREES.COM

WholeTrees is a good example of a Next Economy company that has used segmenting, targeting, and positioning to grow its business. WholeTrees designs, fabricates, and constructs commercial structures made from round timber. When trees are left round, they are 50 percent stronger than milled lumber of the same diameter, as strong as steel in tension, and perform better in fire than both these alternatives. WholeTrees products sequester carbon while avoiding the pollution and carbon that would otherwise be emitted by using steel and concrete. The round timber is sourced from sustainably managed forests and supplied to construction job sites via regional forestry and fabrication networks.

WholeTrees had a choice to make about how to sell its products. The company first focused on people who are involved in choosing what materials to use in the design and construction of buildings. However, this segment still included a broad array of stakeholders, including homeowners, contractors, developers, designers, engineers, and architects. After some trial and error, WholeTrees chose to target and position the company's products to architects. Architects are at the beginning of the design cycle and can create a vision for a building that features the beauty of the round timber. This positioning has

(continued)

Differentiation and Collaboration

In a BAU context, strategic positioning is usually framed as how you can "beat the competition" or "put competitors out of business." How do we enter into a marketplace where there might be other Next Economy companies? Is there a way to complement each other rather than compete? The BAU concept of differentiation is important. Differentiation involves identifying and communicating the unique qualities of your product, service, or company while highlighting the distinct differences between your offerings and those of "competitors." Product differentiation goes hand in hand with developing a strong value proposition so that a product or service is attractive to a target market or audience. In a Next Economy context, there are often unseen benefits to exploring how values-aligned businesses can fit together while still differentiating their unique offerings. This opens the potential to become strategic partners, share best practices, refer work back and forth, and collaborate on expanding your market and network. Collaboration between Next Economy businesses can be critical in order to generate market demand for ideas that are categorically marginalized or excluded. Collaboration also prevents monopolies and ensures a diverse ecosystem of options to meet different needs.

For example, when LIFT Partner Shawn Berry became a worker-owner at a woodworking cooperative earlier in his career, he was struck by the open and enthusiastic reception he would receive when he called other cooperatives for advice, guidance, and sharing best practices. If he called more traditional for-profit companies with similar requests, they would often rebuff him, ignore him, or refuse to share information with him. Values alignment was the key factor in determining how open the companies were to collaborating.

Efficacy of Different Marketing Strategies

Another important practice for Next Economy companies is to prioritize relational marketing. For example, the most effective and least expensive form of marketing is word of mouth. Word of mouth marketing happens when customers talk about a company's product or service to their friends and family, and to others with whom they have close relationships. Strategic partnerships, another effective marketing technique, happen when two organizations collaborate to create campaigns that are beneficial to both parties. It is a cost-effective way of amplifying your market reach by working with an organization whose products or services complement your own. In some cases (but not all), social media and paid advertising are usually more expensive and less effective. This does not mean you should never spend time and money on advertising and social media. Rather, we encourage you to take a blended approach with several different types of marketing channels. The insight is to spend most of your time and energy on the strategies that have the highest efficacy and the least cost.

Core Value Proposition

The goal of strategic positioning is to make your company and its offerings distinct. The goal of a core value proposition is to articulate that distinction clearly. Your core value proposition can be complemented by a number of messages that describe the benefits of what you are offering. These messages are often crafted for specific audiences. In BAU terms, these might also be described as your core differentiators. In developing your core value proposition, you want to marry what is true about you—your sense of yourself, your gifts, what brings you alive, and your values—and convey that with language that people in your target market would identify with.

Case Study: Native American Natural Foods

TANKABAR.COM

Native American Natural Foods is a great example of a company that has had strong strategic positioning and a compelling core value proposition. NANF launched the first meat bar—The Tanka Bar—in 2007 based on a centuries-old Lakota recipe of dried buffalo meat and fruit. The mission of NANF is to return the buffalo to the land, lives, and economy of Indian people. The company is located on the Pine Ridge Indian Reservation in South Dakota. Pine Ridge is home to the Oglala Lakota people. It is also the poorest place in the United States, has unemployment rates between 65 and 85 percent, and has the lowest life expectancy in the Western Hemisphere, outside Haiti. Through selling their product and returning one million buffalo to their native lands, NANF aims to restore the economic foundation of health and prosperity to more than 40,000 Indian people living on Pine Ridge.

The strategic positioning of NANF is that it is the first and only Native American-owned and -operated meat bar company in the United States. The core value proposition is that by purchasing Tanka Bar products, customers are helping restore the buffalo to their historic significance to Indian people. No other meat bar can compete with the authenticity and impact of NANF's positioning and core value proposition.

NEXT ECONOMY PRINCIPLES REPRESENTED:

- 1 Meet Basic Needs
- 2 Share Ownership
- 4 Support Local Communities
- 8 Regenerate Systems
- 9 Build Movements

Evolution of the Core Value Proposition

One pitfall to avoid is believing that your core value proposition, once identified, is fixed for all time. We have seen many organizations change their core value proposition over time as the market changes. For example, a new competitor in the market might change the dynamics of what prospective customers consider when evaluating your brand. Being willing and able to adapt is important. Another pitfall in core value proposition development is entrepreneurs who want their market to believe something (that potential customers may or may not believe). This dovetails with our earlier section on needs versus known needs. For example, some entrepreneurs skip the step of speaking with folks in their market to get their thoughts, feedback, and advice on potential products or services. It can be a humbling experience to do the hard work of defining your core value proposition and differentiating your brand, only to realize that potential customers do not resonate with your messaging.

Example Scenario

A participant in one of our live MBA courses asked a great question related to this topic: "If my customers want environmentally sustainable products, but not something else that I care about—like racial justice—should I switch my targeting to a smaller market that cares about both, or should I try to educate my current market?" In our experience, the first step would be to ensure that you are doing diligent market research and having conversations with clients, customers, and prospective customers to identify their known needs. If you identify a market niche that says they want products that have both a racial justice and an environmental component, then you would position your products to serve that market. On the other hand, if you cannot find evidence that that market niche exists, you could still provide environmentally friendly products, but you could also begin educating your customers about racial justice in order to build a market that is interested in both.

In BAU terminology, creating a market from scratch is usually considered a multimillion-dollar problem. It can be very difficult to create market demand. However, the creative twist we have seen from several organizations is to offer educational services for which people are willing to pay. This allows you to grow your market while sustaining your effort through education services.

Understanding Business as Usual Finance

Another extremely important topic to consider under the larger umbrella of strategy is why, when, and how to raise money for your enterprise. This is a very fraught and misunderstood topic. For example, a number of Next Economy entrepreneurs have told us that they need to raise venture capital. This is different from "I'm looking for fundraising" or "I might need access to capital." Saying "I need to raise venture capital" is a warning sign for us because of the way venture capital is typically structured. It is often not conducive to the impact outcomes that many Next Economy entrepreneurs want to have.

Venture Capital

Venture capital (also referred to as venture private equity) is typically structured as a partnership, a legal entity made up of a general partner and limited partners. A venture capital firm, or "VC," manages the

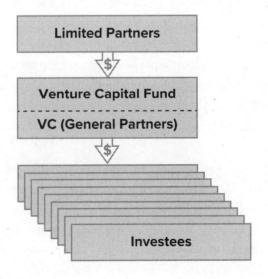

FIGURE 9. The VC Model
Source: Lift Economy

general partner entity, pursues investment opportunities, and seeks to ensure a high return on investment of the fund (see Figure 9). Well-known VCs include Kleiner Perkins, Sequoia Capital, Backstage Capital, Collaborative Fund, and GV (formerly known as Google Ventures). Limited partners, or "LPs," invest in the VCs fund with an expectation of an attractive return for their investment. LPs include public pension funds, corporate pension funds, insurance companies, family offices of high-net-worth individuals, for example Harvard University, the California Public Employees Retirement Plan, Children's Hospital Oakland, and the Bill & Melinda Gates Foundation.

How VC Funds Work

The first key insight to take away from this section is that VCs do not typically invest much (or any) of their own money. VCs almost always raise money from LPs before they can make an investment in a company. This is important because it creates constraints on the types of companies in which a VC firm can invest. As a hypothetical to drive this point home, let's pretend a VC firm approaches executives at the California Public Employees' Retirement Plan (CalPERS) and the Harvard University endowment. Both of these are prospective LPs, because they are multibillion-dollar institutions that invest a portion of the funds that they manage in venture capital. The VC pitches CalPERS and Harvard on a new $500 million fund they are raising. CalPERS and Harvard ask questions like "What is the focus of the fund?" and "What is the expected return on investment?" and "When can we expect to get our money back?" The VC responds that it is a startup fund that—within seven to ten years—they hope will quintuple the amount of any investments made.

At this point the VC has not made investments into any companies. However, the VC's stated return expectations and time frame have already created a number of constraints about what is possible. For example, in order to be able to pay back their LPs the amount they are promising, venture capital firms have to look for investments with the potential to have very high growth and an "exit" or "liquidity event" at a high valuation in a short amount of time. A liquidity event, in financial terms, means an acquisition, merger, initial public offering (IPO), or other action that allows founders and early investors in a company to "exit" (or cash out) some or all of their ownership shares. Exiting is necessary for VC firms because they cannot pay back their LPs without an event that allows them to turn their "illiquid" (or non-tradeable) ownership shares into "liquid" cash. This means that VCs are only looking for companies that are growing rapidly, have a clear exit strategy, have the potential for high profit margins, and operate in a billion-dollar or a multibillion-dollar market (such as software, biotech, etc.).

The Effects of VCs on Startup Culture

Companies that are trying to grow fast at all costs are risky and subject to instability. This is tragic because it has influenced startup culture. We often hear people say, "Startups are inherently risky," or something to the effect of "Nine out of ten startups will fail." It is true that starting a company often requires risk taking. However, the idea that nine out of ten startups will fail could be a culturally determined phenomenon. It is not written in stone that the vast majority of startups fail. It is a pattern that has been heavily influenced by the prodigious promises that venture capital firms make. This is part of the structural dysfunction of the BAU economy.

Reasons to Avoid VCs

You are generally excluded from investment consideration from VCs if you start a company that is creating great vocational pathways for formerly incarcerated folks, if you are a worker-owner at a local cooperative grocery store, or if you are a farmer practicing regenerative agriculture. You can waste a tremendous amount of time as an entrepreneur talking to VCs because your enterprise is probably never going to fit their return expectations. Even if a VC does invest in your company, they might seek to wrest away control and bypass the values or impacts that you wanted to create in the name of creating outsized returns. This continues the practice of concentrating wealth into existing centers of power—typically wealthy white men. As with the rest of society, there are also forces of systemic white supremacy and patriarchy at play, meaning companies founded by women and people of color receive investment from VC firms at a very low rate.

VCs Should Rarely Be Your First Fundraising Stop

There is a very narrow slice of the world of venture capital that does specifically look to invest in women, folks of color, and other under-represented groups. These firms might be values aligned with you—but they are mostly still looking for the same high growth in investment opportunities as all the other VCs. We want to be clear that there are multiple options for raising money. Venture capital is rarely the first place to look. Unfortunately, the normalization of venture capital return and liquidity expectations has heavily influenced the entire culture of early-stage investing—such as with "angel investors" (individuals using their own money to invest).

Order of Operations for Seeking Finance

The following order of operations is not a strict rule that you have to follow. It is meant to be a checklist or set of recommendations to help you retain the greatest amount of control over the impact you desire to make in the world. Here are the five steps we recommend:

1. Customers

The first step is to generate enough profit or revenue from your customers or clients so that you can reinvest in growing the business. This might seem very obvious. However, we have encountered entrepreneurs who believe they need to raise money before they have considered whether they actually need outside capital to move forward. The process of generating all your funding directly from customers is also sometimes referred to as "bootstrapping." We see overcorrections in both directions. Some entrepreneurs and teams (often women and people of color) assume they have to bootstrap as the only way to make it. Others bypass this step and immediately assume they need to raise capital from investors.

2. Suppliers and Vendors

The second step is to look at suppliers and vendors. This is especially relevant for people who are creating goods. For example, you could go to your suppliers and ask them to advance the supplies that are needed to create the goods. Then, once you sell the goods to your customer, you would pay back the supplier. In addition to potentially providing more favorable terms, some of your suppliers may have the cash capacity to invest directly into your business. You might get better terms from a supplier who invests directly because they stand to benefit from your success. If your business does well, you will be buying more supply from them over the long run.

3. Non-Dilutive Capital

"Non-dilutive" capital does not reduce your ownership (or the amount of ownership of the existing stakeholders) in the business. Examples of non-dilutive capital include loans (which we will discuss more in the next part), grants, and philanthropy.

- **Philanthropic donations:** For-profit social enterprises are able to accept donations directly, but they are not able to offer a tax deduction to the donor (only registered 501(c)(3) charities can offer a tax write-off).

- **Program-related investments (PRI) and mission-related investments (MRI):**
  - Some foundations use PRI to support their charitable activities. However, unlike philanthropic grants, PRI are often expected to be paid back, usually at below-market rates. Foundations must assert that the purpose of a PRI investment is not to maximize investment return.
  - MRI are investments that support the mission of the foundation by generating a positive social or environmental impact, while generating reasonably competitive rates of financial return.
  - PRI and MRI can be in the form of non-dilutive capital (like a loan) or they can be in the form of an equity investment

(which would be dilutive). In our experience, even though PRI and MRI can be dilutive, the investments are often structured to be entrepreneur friendly. If you do choose to pursue PRI or MRI capital, note that it can take foundations 12–18 months or more to make a decision about whether to move forward with the investment.

4. Community Capital

Raising capital from your friends, family, local community, and the general public is a great option. However, it is important to be aware of how positionality and intersectionality (such as gender, race, ethnicity, and other forms of identity) affect one's ability to raise investment capital. For example, many folks seeking capital may get advice that they should start with a "friends and family round" when they start raising money. However, due to the legacies of enslavement, genocide, and systemic racism, many Black, Indigenous, and other folks of color do not have access to friends and family with excess cash to invest. RUNWAY is a 100 percent Black- and Brown-women-led organization that is seeking to address this gap. RUNWAY is a financial innovation firm committed to dismantling systemic barriers and reimagining financial policies and practices—all in the name of Black liberation. The organization's work helps build Black community wealth through early-stage funding, holistic business support, and innovative financial products and partnerships.

Going to your broader community, or the general public, can be a strategy to address these structural biases. These are some options:

- **Investment crowdfunding** (including Direct Public Offerings): Many people are familiar with rewards-based crowdfunding, popularized by sites like Kickstarter and Indiegogo. In this model, a large number of people contribute money to support the launch of a new product or service. In return, folks who contribute money receive a T-shirt, small gift, or other perk. With investment crowdfunding, instead of a small perk, you could provide loan terms of repayment or shares of ownership in the company. The investment crowdfunding approach allows you to target a larger number of potential investors who do not necessarily need a certain return on investment. They might be more aligned and more inspired by the vision, mission, and purpose of your organization. As investors, they would be heavily incentivized to become patrons and support your organization. Sites like Crowdfund MainStreet and Wefunder are popular platforms that help facilitate investments.

- **Private community offering:** It is possible to raise investment funding from customers, community members, and fans without an investment crowdfunding campaign. Each state's rules are different, but generally you can raise funding from 10 to 35 investors as long as you do not publicly advertise.

5. Private Equity

Private equity is at the end of our order of operations. The big division between types of private equity is whose money is being invested.

- **Angel investors:** An angel investor is a high-net-worth individual who provides financial backing for small startups or entrepreneurs, typically in exchange for ownership equity in the company. Angels are investing with their own money, so they may be willing to be more flexible with the structure and type of investment. Some angel investors might be willing to accept a lower financial return if they know they're investing in an enterprise that will produce positive social and environmental impacts.

- **Venture capital:** As we described at length in the previous section, "Understanding Business as Usual Finance," traditional venture capital is typically not conducive to, and can be outright antithetical to, the impact outcomes that Next Economy entrepreneurs want to have. That is why it is last on our recommended order of operations. However, we want to be clear that it is possible to create social and environmental impact with venture capital finance. There are some venture capital firms, such as Radicle Impact, Raven Indigenous Capital Partners, Cienega Capital, and Fledge, that are committed to using the VC model to benefit society and the environment.

Next Steps on Raising Capital

In sum, we highly recommend that you put some serious thought into what kind of impact you want to create in the community and which capital raising strategies might give you the best chance at achieving those goals. For example, you might grow as much as you can from generating revenue. Then you take out a loan. You might follow that up with an investment crowdfunding campaign. You might be able to get all the resources you need without having to relinquish control of your company or being forced to sacrifice your impact in order to achieve hyper growth. However, there might be a scenario where you have checked off the first three steps on our order of operations. Once you have a market and traction and you are ready to expand, you might choose to pursue venture capital investment. The key at this point would be to try, as much as possible, to seek investment from VC firms that are impact-oriented and mission-aligned. For more on the topic of raising mission-aligned capital, we recommend *Raise Capital on Your Own Terms: How to Fund Your Business Without Selling Your Soul* by Jenny Kassan (National Geographic Books, 2017).

Security Structure Options

What is a "security" and how does it relate to financing for your business? There is a lot of confusing jargon in the world of raising capital: Equity, Debt, Royalty, Revenue Share, Dividends, Integrated Capital. You are not alone if you feel overwhelmed by this topic. The financial system and the language that is used to describe it is often opaque, confusing, and off putting. Our goal is to present some of the fundamental information you need, while also providing resources for those of you who want to go deeper. We want to empower entrepreneurs to create an offering that fits their vision, values, and needs—then look for investors who are a fit (rather than conforming to prevailing investment norms).

It should be noted that the authors of this book are not credentialed legal professionals. Nothing shared in this topic should be construed by you as legal advice. We highly recommend that you speak with an attorney to ensure any financing strategy you pursue is compliant with local laws and regulations. Please see the LIFT website (lifteconomy. com/mbabook) for recommendations on attorneys and other resources related to this topic. Here are some basic definitions of common terms:

Security

A security is a financial instrument or asset. It is typically associated with investing money into something with the idea of getting something (often money, but it does not have to be money) back in exchange. In the United States, offering a security and soliciting investment in your enterprise is regulated at both the federal and state levels.

Equity

When people talk about investments they are usually thinking of equity. Equity, as used here, refers to the ownership of an entity. In a corporation, it usually means who owns shares of stock in the company. The owners are the ones who reap the benefits when an entity generates profits or from a sale of the entity's assets. It is important to note that ownership is not the same thing as control (or governance). The owners of an entity may be in control, but not always. For example, due to poor management, some founders of startups have been removed from day-to-day operational control of a company they founded. These founders still retain their ownership (and rights to any profits), but they no longer have control over decisions made at the company.

- *Advantages:* An equity investment is most often structured so that the financial returns to investors are contingent on the creation of a surplus or profit in the future. For example, you might sell 20 percent of your company to investors. You could use their investment money today and not be expected to pay them back until a later date. This is in contrast to a loan (which we will describe later in this chapter), where you usually have to make a recurring interest payment to pay down the debt regardless of the financial stability of your company.

- *Disadvantages:* Raising equity can be associated with partial loss of control over the company. Corporate entities are structured with the idea that voting power is proportional to the total number of shares. Another disadvantage is that your relationship with equity investors may be for the entire life of the business. For example, you might pay back 10 to 20 times the amount they originally invested. There are ways to build in structured exits so that this is not always the case.

  It is possible to include terms of redemption related to offering equity in exchange for investment. Redemption can mean that the organization has the option to repurchase (or redeem) the equity shares that were purchased by the inventors. Repurchase usually happens after a certain period and at a predefined "multiple cap" on the original investment. The multiple cap sets a maximum for the price paid when redeeming the equity shares to limit the potential return of the investor. For example, a multi-cap term might set the option to redeem the equity shares at twice the original investment amount after eight years. This type of term allows the company to plan to have cash or raise other capital. The benefit is that they will be able to provide an exit for the investors and retain control and ownership by the company and its other stakeholders.

Traditional Debt (Loans)

Debt is an obligation that requires one party to pay money or other agreed-upon value to another party. Loans, bonds, promissory notes, and mortgages are all types of debt. For example, you might take out a bank loan and make regular interest and principal payments until the loan is paid off. Debt may be owed by a sovereign state or country, local government, company, or an individual.

- *Advantages:* Debt is non-dilutive, which means you do not have to give up ownership. In addition, once you pay off a loan, you are done with that investor. You do not have to worry about them still being involved past the repayment date. Debt can also have a flexible structure. It does not have to be regular increasing principal payments with decreasing interest payments until the loan is paid off. For example, you might get a 10-year loan that is interest-only for the first three years (to allow you time to build up your business) and then principal plus interest for the remaining seven years. Debt can be long term, such as 10, 20, or 30 years and more.

- *Disadvantages:* Debt lenders often require borrowers to have "collateral" to "secure" the loan. This is often in the form of personal assets (house, car, savings account, etc.), which means that if you are not able to pay the lender back, the lender can seize your house or car (or whatever you used as collateral) in order to offset their losses from your defaulting on the loan. This policy has racialized implications. With the history of racial segregation and marginalization, many Black, Indigenous, and other folks of color do not have generational wealth or assets that can be used as collateral for loans. "Unsecured" loans, which do not require collateral, have been used to address this racial disparity.

Case Study: Seed Commons   SEEDCOMMONS.ORG

Seed Commons is a national network of locally rooted, non-extractive loan funds that brings the power of finance under community control. Seed Commons channels investment to marginalized communities that have borne the brunt of the extractive economy, deindustrialization, and systemic discrimination. The organization makes local, community-controlled finance available to cooperatively owned businesses that create jobs, build wealth, and challenge inequality. Almost 100 percent of their lending is to worker cooperatives.

Seed Commons practices non-extractive financing. The idea behind non-extraction is that the borrower should never be worse off than before they received the loan (i.e., the returns to the lender should never exceed the wealth created by the borrower using the capital).

(continued)

Case Study: Seed Commons *(continued)*

Some examples of their non-extractive lending terms:

- *No repayments greater than profits:* Borrowers are not required to make interest or principal repayments until they are able to cover operating costs, including market-rate salaries.

- *No personal guarantees:* Repayment will not be extracted from prior existing business assets or the personal assets of those who make up the enterprise. Collateral will be restricted to items purchased *with financing from Seed Commons.*

- *No credit scores:* Instead of credit scores, Seed Commons uses close relationships between local loan officers and potential loan recipients to establish a borrower's reliability.

- Seeds Commons is building a key part of the infrastructure necessary for a truly just, democratic, and sustainable Next Economy.

NEXT ECONOMY PRINCIPLES REPRESENTED:

- 2 Share Ownership
- 3 Democratize Governance
- 4 Support Local Communities
- 6 Promote Open Source
- 10 Build Movements

Royalties and Revenue Sharing

"Royalty on revenues" or "revenue sharing" or "revenue-based finance" structures are based on the idea of trying to align incentives to the success or the growth of the company. You can have revenue-based equity and/or revenue-based debt structures. To illustrate, let's say someone invests into your company. As your company generates revenue, the revenue-sharing agreement is that you will pay back the investor a small percentage (e.g., 2 percent) of all the revenue your company generates. The agreement states that you will make annual payments until the investor gets paid back some capped multiple (e.g., twice, three times) their original investment. Then you are considered to have paid back the loan in full, and you no longer have other obligations to that investor.

- *Advantages:* The advantage of a royalty on revenue model is that the amount you owe back to the investor each year is correlated with how much revenue you generate. If you made zero revenue in the first year, your payment back to the investor is zero. If you generated $10,000, and your agreed payment is 2%, you would pay them $200. You would keep making payments like this until you repaid the investor the capped multiple of their original investment.

- *Disadvantages:* The challenge with seeking a royalty on revenue structure is that it is still relatively uncommon, and not many investors know about it or are comfortable with it. There may be some degree of difficulty in the cost of your time and legal costs. If you plan on raising more money later (e.g., more debt or equity), it can make it more complicated or challenging to raise capital in a different security structure. Another disadvantage is if you don't put a limit, or "cap," on your revenue-sharing agreement (e.g., once the investor gets double their original investment, they are considered paid in full), then an investor might continue to take a percentage of your revenue in perpetuity.

Dividends

Dividends are associated with a share of the ownership, and thus some share of the company's profits. However, the amount of dividends paid out to shareholders usually depends on "net profit" or "net income" (i.e., the amount of profit that remains after all expenses and costs have been subtracted from the company's revenue). In contrast, a royalty on revenue debt structure would typically pay the investor back regardless of how much net profit or net income was made. Annual net earnings of a company do not necessarily need to be paid out as dividends. The company may want to retain the earnings to build up a cash reserve, invest in new products or services, or invest in growing their impact.

Integrated Capital

Integrated capital is the coordinated use of different forms of financial capital and nonfinancial resources to support a social enterprise. It might involve loans, equity investments, grants, technical assistance, network connections, and more. The benefit of integrated capital is that it can unlock other forms of investment by making the opportunity seem less risky. For example, when the LIFT Economy team was seeking to raise $1,000,000 for the Force for Good Fund, we simultaneously sought to raise $100,000 in philanthropic donations as a "loss reserve" for the fund. The goal of the loss reserve was to provide investors with some confidence that if our fund did not do as well as anticipated (e.g., we invested $1,000,000 but only got $900,000 back), we had $100,000 we could use to make them whole again. This somewhat de-risked our fund in the mind of investors and helped unlock more investment capital into the Force for Good Fund. The idea for the loan loss reserve came from the Pioneer Valley Grows Investment Fund (PVGIF).

Case Study: Force for Good Fund
LIFTECONOMY.COM/FORCEFORGOOD

LIFT Economy, Jenny Kassan, and Community Ventures launched the Force for Good Fund in 2016. The goal of the Force for Good Fund was to help nurture, support, and grow women- and people-of-color-owned companies that were creating an outsized positive social and environmental impact. This fund was needed because it was, and still is, incredibly difficult for early-stage, socially and environmentally responsible businesses run by women and people of color to access non-extractive capital. In addition to financial support, the fund provided consulting support and technical assistance to investees. The Force for Good Fund ultimately raised $1.1M from

(continued)

135 people and invested in 13 businesses. Some of the investees included Tanka Resilient Agriculture Cooperative (Kyle, SD), the East Bay Permanent Real Estate Cooperative (Oakland, CA), The Guild (Atlanta, GA), Our Table Cooperative (Sherwood, OR), and Red Bay Coffee (Oakland, CA).

NEXT ECONOMY PRINCIPLES REPRESENTED:

- 2 Share Ownership
- 5 Integrate Education
- 6 Promote Open Source
- 7 Embody Transparency
- 8 Regenerate Systems
- 10 Build Movements

The Importance of a Compliance Strategy

You need a compliance strategy if you are thinking about raising money (regardless of whether it is debt, royalty on revenue, equity, or something else). A compliance strategy will help you identify how you can raise money within the existing laws and regulations in your area. We want to reiterate our recommendation that you should seek legal advice before structuring your security. An attorney can help you be thoughtful about which type of security you choose, not just to raise money in the short term, but the implications of different types of structures on your ability to raise capital in the future.

Finding Investors

Now that you understand your options for raising capital, how do you go about finding people who are willing to invest? There are a few things to consider when trying to find the right investors. You want to qualify investors by understanding their area of focus, the types of investments they typically make, and their process. You also want to learn how to have conversations with them and how to close the deal.

Qualifying Investors

Taking time to qualify your investors is a very important process. It is prework for you to do before going out and having conversations. It is a way to hone and focus your approach before you expend a lot of time and energy. See the workbook for a list of questions that you can use as a checklist for qualifying investors. The more you know, the more likely you will be to find out if they are a fit for your investment opportunity or not.

Communicating with Investors

Once you have qualified an investor, how do you strike up a conversation? Do you use LinkedIn? Do you call and leave a voicemail? Do you send a cold email? The most successful way to engage with an investor is to have somebody they already know introduce you to them. If you know someone who knows the investor (and is willing to make the introduction), you could use the following email template to reach out. The same email template can work if you are reaching out to community investors, experienced investors, and/or professional investors.

> Hi _____. Per our discussion, I'm hoping you would be able to facilitate a connection between me and _____ (investor). For ease, could you please forward this email as an introduction and CC me? Here is the context for which we discussed that a connection would be mutually beneficial (insert two to four sentences about what the company does, the impact it creates, and why this person might be a good fit). Thanks for the introduction!

If you don't know anyone who knows the investor, that is fine. You can try to contact them in whatever way is possible. The key is to keep it short and sweet. Don't send them the entire pitch deck. Try to communicate to the investor that you have done some of the research and prequalification to ensure that the investment opportunity would be a good fit. This way they will perceive you as less likely to waste their time.

Agreeing on Fit

The first signal you are looking for when talking to an investor is that they are interested, and they believe it could be a fit. You are looking for some language like "This fits with my investment thesis" or "You are at the right stage, and I could imagine us going to the next steps." You don't have to ask them if they are going to write a check tomorrow. The key is seeing if they are interested in potentially making an investment.

Sprint to Paper

The next milestone in the process is getting to the terms of the investment. An investor might tell you what needs to happen in order for them to invest. We recommend writing what they say down and using it as a project plan. If you do not effectively manage this process, the time from "Yes, we are interested in investing" to a check sent is where the biggest lags can happen. Once you have an agreement (sometimes referred to as a term sheet) in hand, it is important to carefully review the investment terms before agreeing to them. Do the terms actually make sense for your business? Are these the terms you agreed upon in previous conversations?

Getting the Check

It can be very exciting to get a signed agreement from an investor. You might think this is the last step and that the check is in the mail. Unfortunately, that is not always the case. The investor might ask for still more information, want to talk to their lawyer one last time, delay in getting your wire transfer information, and so on. Similar to the step above, you want to manage the process by asking them to disclose what exact steps are required to get the check. Write those steps down and recycle that information back to the investor to hold them accountable.

Final Thoughts on Finding Investors

As you can see, you can waste a tremendous amount of time not being organized or diligent about finding the right type of investors. The sooner you can get to the question "Is this something you would be interested in potentially investing in?" the sooner you will be able to qualify them. It may have only required you to spend 45 minutes talking with an investor to get to a no. This will allow you to spend more time speaking with other folks that have the potential to invest. Remember, no is a better answer than "Maybe," "We are still thinking about it," or "Good meeting." If they showed interest in your company, but declined to invest, ask them if they know any other investors who would be a good fit for your stage and the impact you are creating in the world.

Decision-Making and Governance

The following sections move away from finance and introduce the topics of decision-making, governance, and partnerships. Decision-making and governance are nested under "Part 7: Strategy" (as opposed to "Part 8: Operational Systems") because how your company makes decisions, how responsibility and authority are delegated, how proposals are generated, and the like, are all strategic choices. This includes better understanding why people meet and how to best use that time effectively.

Reasons to Meet

One of the best reasons to meet is to make decisions between available alternatives. Making decisions is a very important component of creating shared power and a more equitable and democratic culture. Two of the most common ways of making decisions are simple majority voting (the majority wins and the minority loses) and consensus (everyone must agree in order to move forward). What is surprising to many people is that these are not the only two options—it is a spectrum. The spectrum of decision-making options spans supermajority voting, consent, modified consensus (also known as consensus-minus-one), advice process, and more.

Delegation: Who Is Actually Making What Decisions?

Many egalitarian organizations require consent or consensus on every decision. This is a very high standard to meet and can bog down decision-making. Decision zone charts can be a helpful tool to get more efficient and streamlined. In a decision zone chart, you list the different stakeholder groups, identify what kind of decisions they might make, and identify the method and mechanism they use to make those decisions. Creating a decision zone chart (see Figure 10) that delegates authority and power could require a consensus vote. However, that one-time consensus vote would set up a lot of organizational efficiency by directing any future decisions into categories that are predetermined.

ROLE	RESPONSIBILITY & DECISION-MAKING AUTHORITY	MECHANISM
Member-owners	• Set vision, mission, and culture • Elect Board of Directors • Vote on key decisions • Approve new hires	Modified Consensus
Board of Directors	• Set strategy to accomplish vision and mission • Set company goals • Review reporting • Hire, appoint, direct, and supervise management	Modified Consensus
Management	• Implement strategy to achieve company goals • Declare need for new hires • Recruit, select, orient, and train new hires • Conduct performance enhancements • Receive reporting from team leads • Monitor and assist team leads • Prepare and monitor annual budget • Monitor cash flow	Advice Process
Team Leads	• Team membership and team roles • Create and implement strategy for projects • Report to management on team performance • Monitor and assist team members	Advice Process
Team Members	• Assist in the creation of project strategy • Execute on tasks • Manage individual workload	Self-management

FIGURE 10. Example of Decision Zones for a Cooperative
Source: Lift Economy

Crafting Effective Proposals

In our experience, there is a lack of skill and experience in the formulation of a proposal or a choice between alternatives. Many folks doing collective decision-making tend to excessively analyze, assess, and express their internal experiences. The LIFT team often writes the words "I propose that…" in view of participants when we facilitate meetings. "I propose that…" is a powerful forcing function to help move the conversation past the expression of your internal experience to a choice between alternatives. There is a natural tendency to avoid this type of language because there is a fear that your proposal might be rejected. However, without proposing a choice between alternatives, meetings could go on for a long time.

Broadening Your Range of Tolerance

Many people, including those working in cooperatives and communitarian organizations, want to only support decisions with which they are perfectly aligned. As you might imagine, this is not conducive to efficient decision-making processes. We use the question "Is it workable?" as a cut-through to determine if someone can tolerate moving forward with a certain decision or tolerate it for long enough so it can be tested. It is very rare that any proposal in any group larger than a few people is going to be perfectly acceptable to all participants. Oftentimes, a participant will have some objection to some aspect of the proposal. Building up the habit of determining whether a proposal is workable is key to more effective decision-making and governance. See the chart in Figure 11 for an illustration of "The Range of Tolerance."

The Seven Stages of Cooperativism

Many, perhaps most, people were raised in families where they were not involved in making any collective decisions. The parents and caregivers made decisions, the schools and teachers decided what to study, and now employers dictate what is allowed or not. A lack of experience in collective decision-making is not your fault. You are situated within

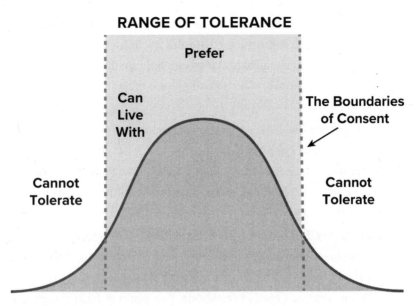

RANGE OF TOLERANCE

Prefer

Can Live With

The Boundaries of Consent

Cannot Tolerate

Cannot Tolerate

FIGURE 11. The Range of Tolerance
Source: Lift Economy

a hierarchical culture. The seven stages of cooperativism illustrate how someone typically moves through their understanding of cooperative governance process.

- **Stage 1:** *I do not trust this process.* Usually people sit back, observe, and refrain from participating when they are first invited into a collective process.

- **Stage 2:** *I kind of care about this. I am going to try putting my voice in once.* Over time, if enough trust and rapport is built up, someone may try to add their voice to the discussion. Next Economy organizations will typically celebrate this participation and encourage the individual to keep sharing.

- **Stage 3:** *Wow, people listen to me!* The third stage is when people start to get excited about having agency in the decision-making process.

- **Stage 4:** *Hey, I like this power, I am going to weigh in on every-thing.* People realize that they have the power to affect decisions. They might suddenly start caring about every agenda item, such as the color the signs are painted, the font used on the website, the types of clothing allowed at work, the brand of copier paper, and so on. They realize that they can hold up the entire meeting for months because it feels good to have their voice heard.

- **Stage 5:** *These meetings take forever!* When the next stage hits, folks might feel like cooperation is so slow and inefficient. The meetings are like pulling teeth. They are done with it. Sometimes this stage can come in parallel with their own tendency to weigh in on every decision. The next stage is a breakthrough in efficacy and efficiency.

- **Stage 6:** *OK, I am going to add my voice more selectively.* In this stage, you realize that you do not need to weigh in on everything. You decide to add your voice occasionally to things that you really care about. You begin to trust the group to make decisions that work for the collective. In some ways this can feel like resignation, but often feels like liberation as you grow in discernment about where you want to exercise your governance power.

- **Stage 7:** *I am going to facilitate this journey for others.* In the final stage, you realize that collective decision-making is a really important social technology, and that you want to hold space for the journey through cooperativism for others.

We offer this framework because people are entering into communitarian or cooperative processes at different stages of experience. This is a diagnostic tool to better understand where someone might be on this journey and to help people move to the next stage.

Strategic Partnerships

Partnerships can help you with your strategy for providing your organization's goods and services. When cooperatives, nonprofits, and other social enterprises come to us when they are running into roadblocks and potential points of failure, we often ask them to describe their partnership strategy (who they are thinking of partnering with and what mutual value the two organizations might create). For example, if a client organization thinks they need to spend more money on advertising in order to increase their sales and distribution, we first prompt them to describe who they are partnering with to get the word out and/or to get their product distributed. A lot of clients do not have a partnership strategy. We help them formulate this and make it an integral part of their business. It is supportive of the Next Economy (specifically Next Economy Principle 4: Support Local Communities) to cultivate local partnerships for supply, distribution, banking, or other services. Sourcing locally is counter to the BAU trend of outsourcing your services to exploited labor in some other country.

Getting Invited In: The Key to Building Solid Partnerships

Business-to-business relationships are not the only type of partnerships. We often encourage companies to look at what grassroots, activist, and community-based organizations could provide mutually beneficial value. As a brainstorming exercise, try to make a list of a few grassroots organizations that intersect with your vision. Once you have identified several organizations, the next step is figuring out the best way to reach out, establish a connection, and build trust. Starhawk, an author, activist, permaculture designer, and teacher, has told members of the LIFT team that "you can only be helpful if you are invited in." Instead of asking how you can help, Starhawk encourages groups to ask how they can get invited. This is a different question that might require different actions. There are many stories, especially about white people and white-led organizations, of those who intend to help but end up causing harm. Remember that relationships grow at the speed of trust. The invitation will emerge when the right level of trust and rapport has been established.

8

Operational Systems

The last component of designing your enterprise includes creating an organizational structure, roles, responsibilities, and tasks; creating a financial projection (i.e., expected revenues, expenses, and cash flows of a business over a forecast period); instituting policies and procedures; and improving your personal productivity systems. Getting your vision, culture, strategy, and operational systems locked in gives your organization a very good chance of creating a long-term positive impact on society and the environment.

Organizational Structure, Roles, and Tasks

Once you have some traction on your strategic development, you can justify investing in developing the operational systems that will determine how the company functions on an ongoing basis. Policies and procedures need to be documented in order to train and delegate to other team members as the organization grows.

Operational Structure

There can be tension in developing operational structures (putting together an organizational chart, creating financial projections, assigning roles and accountabilities, etc.) as they can be seen as "big company stuff" and not essential to the important tasks at hand. While it is important not to overinvest in systems creation, there is also risk involved with underinvesting. You can develop a coherent system of organizational development that balances intentional design with the organic growth of the enterprise. You want to build new systems as they are needed to create clarity and improve performance.

Organizational Chart

One key element of your operational structure is a chart or diagram of the organization that indicates the major groupings of functions and tasks and who is involved. This is often called an "org chart" (see the example in Figure 12). The main purpose of the org chart is to be a visual representation of the whole organization for shared understanding and collaboration. This chart should capture all areas of activity in the organization and how they relate to each other as a whole. It should also represent who is on the team and the areas in which they are working. This can be crucial to define "who is doing what." The org chart structure of defining who is accountable can also extend through job descriptions, chart of accounts, budgets (labor and cash), meeting agendas, reporting, organization rhythms, goals, governance, time planning, tracking, file storage, and more.

DESIGN			
	VISION	CULTURE	STRATEGY	OPERATIONS
Lead	Kevin	Ryan	Erin	Shawn
Support 1	Erin	Erin	Shawn	Kevin

REVENUE			
	MARKETING	SALES	DELIVERY	SERVICE
Lead	Jeanette	GAP	Erin	Erin
Support 1	Ryan	Shawn	Shawn	Ryan
Support 2	Emmy	Emmy	Kevin	Emmy
Support 3			Ryan	
Support 4			Phoenix	
Support 5			Emmy	

ADMIN			
	IT	OFFICE	ACCOUNTING	LEGAL
Lead	Ryan	GAP	Kevin	Ryan
Support 1	Kevin	Ryan	Shawn	Kevin

FIGURE 12. Example Organizational Chart
Source: Lift Economy

Distinctions in Our Org Chart

You may have seen similar charts before, as many companies use them. We will highlight a few key distinctions that we think are important for Next Economy organizations. We use the word *Design* at the top level where a traditional company may use the word *Management*. There is a subtle distinction to invoke the curious exploration of strategies that we can describe as "iterative design," "human-centered design," or "design thinking." This contrasts with "Management," which implies that people know what is going to happen and are managing to conform to expectations.

The other primary distinction is the placement of *Culture* at the top of the chart. In a traditional company this would be called "human resources" and put at the bottom on the Admin level. Relegating culture to an administrative concern is a serious oversight that fails to recognize its fundamental power to influence the success of the organization's efforts. Traditional org charts are usually oriented towards the hierarchy of decision-making authority. This chart is more about wholeness to empower coordinated teamwork and shared understanding. Names on this chart are more about responsibility and accountability and less about status, control, power, and prestige. This chart represents a basic structure that can be adapted and applied to most teams. However, it is far more important that any given team feel empowered to draft a chart that feels uniquely suited to their specific set of circumstances.

The Design Level

The Design level of the org chart can also be thought of as strategy. This level is most concerned with the big picture and the future direction of the organization. The tasks on this level are very important and often not urgent, such as creating your five-year vision, identifying your core values, and setting marketing goals. It can be hard for Next Economy organizations to balance investing in the future of the organization while running the current operations on the Revenue and Admin levels. The Design level includes Vision, Culture, Strategy, and Operational Systems. One of the main interventions in our consulting work is to hold the team's focus on two or three key Design level initiatives. From our experience working with hundreds of social enterprises, we have calculated that spending two percent to five percent of the total staff time on Design can be plenty. Design level initiatives can vary by season and stage of development. However, a rough benchmark is that investing more than five percent of time into the Design level could become too expensive. Less than two percent of time invested in the Design level could not be enough to make needed changes for the future.

The Revenue Level

The Revenue level includes all activities that bring in earned revenue to the organization. This level includes Marketing, Sales, Delivery (of the product or service), and Customer Service. The Delivery org area is the only area where the organization generates revenue—all other areas are cost centers. For most business models, the vast majority of staff time is spent in the Revenue level and specifically in the Delivery area. The money generated in this area has to cover the costs of the goods and services sold (or COGS) and all other overhead expenses incurred by the organization.

The Admin Level

The Admin level accomplishes all the administrative concerns of the organization including Information Technology (IT), Office, Accounting, Facility and Legal (including compliance) concerns. These functions are ideally performed as efficiently and systematically as possible in order to help keep the overhead of the organization low.

Roles and Accountabilities

Clarity of roles, decision-making, and reporting can all be specified through this chart. Once you have the org areas identified, you can identify the Lead and Support staff for each area. The Lead for an area is the one responsible for managing that area, whether they do it themselves or delegate the duties to someone else. The Support backs up the Lead in case they cannot fulfill their duties.

This chart also tends to the creation of specific accountabilities rather than job titles. There are several advantages to this:

- *Clarity of function:* Job titles often mean different things to different people. Assigning Lead and Support roles helps clarify who does what.

- *Ease and efficiency:* Tasks can be evolved and delegated to different people without needing to change job titles. This type of clarity creates efficiency and effectiveness. Your team will better comprehend the overall structure of the organization, who is doing what, and who is empowered to make which decisions.

- *Evolving role description:* Another benefit is this allows creation of a discrete list of regularly occurring tasks for which each team member is responsible. This becomes their current and evolving role description. When you have this in place you can create regular check-ins to ensure your team is meeting its goals.

Evolving Your Tools

It is important for your team to collaborate on refining your org chart (and other tools) as you build your organization. Do not assume you have a perfect structure from the beginning. Also, please feel free to edit (or completely disregard) our org chart. If you want to use our template, make it fit your organization. Edit the language and add or remove areas as needed.

Financial Projections

All Next Economy enterprises need to track and account for the activities of the organization. Financial systems—whether for maintaining compliance with the expectations of BAU reporting requirements (taxes, government, lenders, investors, etc.) or for helping navigate towards the impact outcomes of the organization—can be confusing. Learning them can feel like learning code or a foreign language. This is true even if core aspects of financial systems like "income comes in, expenses go out" are quite intuitive. There may be good reasons for the "coded" approach. The effect is that financial systems—the language of accounting and finance—have been wielded, intentionally or unintentionally, as tools of exclusion and oppression.

Financial Reluctance

Insular knowledge can be powerful, especially when it comes to having control over cash, taxes, payroll, and other matters that are vital to the survival of the organization. As a consequence, many Next Economy entrepreneurs avoid accounting and financial systems altogether or abdicate control to third parties. This can be risky as you are giving away a large amount of power over the organization (and potentially its ability to sustain and function). Others engage reluctantly, not sure where to start and which pieces are important.

Literacy vs. Mastery

What level of understanding is required for Next Economy organizations to embody Next Economy principles? We advocate for universal financial systems *literacy*—not necessarily competence or mastery. We are not saying that everyone in the organization needs to manage the finances. We do say it is important to distribute the literacy and oversight of financial systems broadly within the organization to distribute power in more equitable ways. This might look like every team member having access to (and an understanding of) regular financial reports that they review independently or in a brief team meeting once per week.

Compliance Accounting

You primarily use compliance accounting for taxes and for generating reports for certain stakeholders. Compliance accounting records historical transactions and the present financial status of the organization. It does not look forward in time. Compliance accounting is biased toward purely financial transaction metrics (units sold, revenue collected, bank fees spent, wages, etc.) and does not typically measure other outcomes and impacts (community members served, vocations created, biodiversity increased, greenhouse gas emissions reduced, employees homed after being unhoused, etc.).

Tracking transactions using a system of double entry bookkeeping (a standard method of noting transactions in BAU accounting) can help you easily produce reporting for taxes, statements for investors, information for stakeholders, and for other compliance purposes.

Thankfully, software to support double entry record keeping (such as Xero or QuickBooks) has evolved and is generally accessible. It still can feel intimidating and does appear like code with its own jargon. Specific competence on how to record and categorize transactions is not typically required for everyone. However, as mentioned before, universal basic literacy about the financial statements or reports that can be produced from record keeping can be a critical factor in the long-term success of your company.

Management Accounting

Management accounting is not just interested in the past. It also looks at what is happening in the present moment and what might happen in the future. You use management accounting to help understand the enterprise and what resources might be needed, and to be able to answer certain questions, such as these:

- Can you sustain the organization if you lower your prices to make goods or services more accessible?
- Can you hire more team members? When?
- Can you increase benefits to stakeholders?
- Can you distribute more profit to community stakeholders?
- Can you pick a more socially just supplier or purchase new equipment?
- Can you add a new product or service?

Management accounting practices invite you to ask and answer similar questions that relate to the strategy, mission, and impact of the organization. Similar to financial literacy in compliance accounting, universal literacy in how to interpret reports, statements, and operating projections in a management accounting capacity can be a critical success factor.

Financial Statements

There are three basic financial statements used in the BAU economy for compliance accounting and managerial accounting: the balance sheet, the profit and loss (or income) statement, and the cash flow statement.

These three statements together show the assets and liabilities of a business, its revenues and costs, and its cash flows from operating, investing, and financing activities. Your understanding of these three financial statements is important because they show how your business is operating. They provide insight into how much revenue your business generates, the costs (or expenses) of doing business, how efficiently your business manages its cash, and your company's assets and liabilities. Financial statements provide you with the information you need to assess how well (or poorly) your company is doing.

- *Balance sheet*
  - Provides information about a point in time based on past activities.
  - Useful for understanding the financial position or health of a company by enumerating the assets, liability, and any equity (shareholder equity) in the organization.
  - Important for Next Economy organizations to understand in relation to the profit and loss statement (e.g., a Next Economy organization can be profitable on the profit and loss statement for a period, but not actually be healthy or viable in the long run if the balance sheet shows significant near term and long term liabilities).
  - Important for (or required by) potential investors and lenders.

- *Profit and loss (or income) statement*
  - Presents information from a period of time in the past (can be year to date).
  - The BAU purpose is to tell the story about profitability and is important for taxes and presenting information to investors or creditors.
  - Shows by category where revenue is coming from, what expenses have gone out, and how much of both.
  - Can be very useful when comparing different periods of time to understand what has changed in an organization (e.g., comparing the month of May last year to the month of May this year).

– Can also include impact metrics or ratios for more accessible understanding (e.g., dollars of earned income per program graduate or greenhouse gas emissions reduced per dollar of revenue).

- *Statement of cash flows*
  – Shows the movement of cash over time with an emphasis on cash balance now.
  – One of the more complicated aspects of the coded language of accounting and financial systems is to distinguish between what the profit and loss statement shows and what the cash flow statement shows. It is quite possible to show profit on the profit and loss statement, but for the statement of cash flows to show that the organization will not be able to make payroll or meet other obligations because of lack of available *cash* balance (because of loan principal repayments, for example).
  – Can be perplexing for many Next Economy teams and entrepreneurs and increasing understanding about this can be critical.

Universal basic literacy in how to interpret those three financial statements and how they interact can be important for both intersecting with compliance obligations and making managerial decisions about potential changes. Once you and your team develop a sense for which ratios (financial metrics to impact metrics) best correlate to the impacts that you aspire to create, you can create a dashboard that shares the critical information or key performance indicators with the entire team to regularly access and review.

Constructing Your Financial Projections

An interactive future-oriented financial projection is one of the most critical systems for Next Economy organizations to develop and use. This should be used both to understand the assumptions and elements of the operations of an organization and to create strategies for how to generate beneficial impact.

- *Assumptions*
  - Gather the assumptions that drive your operational model all in one place. These may include financial forecasts about costs, revenue, return on investment, and operating and startup expenses. Financial assumptions serve as a forecast of what your business will do in the future. You need to include them so you have some idea of how accurate your projections may be. For example, when Allbirds went public in November 2021, it noted that the average American purchased seven pairs of shoes per year. One of the company's assumptions was that this trend would continue and provide strong growth for the company. However, when the U.S. economy slowed amid fears of inflation in 2022, people bought fewer pairs of shoes. For this and other reasons, the Allbirds stock price went from about $32 per share in November 2021 to under $3 per share one year later.
  - It is not uncommon for us to see an organization that has priced its offerings for a market below (or too close to) the cost to produce the goods or provide the services (see *Cost of goods sold*). A well-constructed operating projection will highlight this lack of margin by exposing the assumptions.

- *Sales forecast*
  - A sales forecast is a future guess of the monthly sales transactions for each product or service over the next three or more years. Many organizations that we work with do not develop a sales forecast for fear of being wrong (or disappointed in the future). A spreadsheet forecast can allow both a bottom-up, month-by-month educated guess based on historical or present evidence and a top-down forecast. Top-down means using the goals of the organization and "back casting" (working backwards from the end goal) what sales would need to be in order to achieve those goals. An operating projection spreadsheet that automatically links the sales forecast to assumptions of needed resources, capacity, and cost of goods sold can enable you to gut-check answers to such questions as "Do you

have enough people for that level of sales?" and "Is it possible to sell that many goods or services this year in order to approach the goal of providing full benefits to all team members and dividends to community owners?"

- *Cost of goods (or services) sold*
  - Cost of goods sold (COGS) includes all the direct costs that go up or down depending upon how many goods you create or services you provide. For example, the amount of flour purchased by Arizmendi Bakery directly correlates with the number of loaves of bread they make, but their rent expense for the bakery is fixed or an indirect cost and does not fluctuate depending on how much bread is produced. Flour in this case is part of COGS, rent is not.
  - List the COGS for each of the core products or services of your organization in one place in your projection. Many organizations skip this step and discount (or ignore) certain labor inputs (for co-ops, this often is the worker-owners). If you do not list your COGS, you may be pricing your goods or services lower than it costs to make them and your business model may not be feasible in the long run.

- *Fixed expenses or overhead*
  - List all the indirect or fixed expenses (like rent) of the organization in one place. This would include all labor not directly tied to the cost of goods sold and all other overhead. Understanding your fixed expenses is often easier than developing the sales forecast (or analyzing the cost of goods sold) and can usually be formulaically input (using a spreadsheet) into an expense forecast that mirrors the time period of the sales forecast.
  - You may want to treat labor overhead differently than other expenses. Include a variable forecast or a capacity plan that is easy to adjust (adding or subtracting employees in certain roles in the future) that correlates with the sales

forecast. Labor is the greatest expense for most organizations. Answering hypothetical scenario questions about hiring more people is a frequent function of an operating projection.

A well-constructed projection will link the assumptions, the sales forecast, and the expense forecast presented monthly with a cash orientation. This means you put numbers in the sheet aligned with actual "cash in" and "cash out" rather than what is called "accrual notation." Accrual means that you recognize (record the numbers of) a transaction (revenue or expense) at the time of the revenue or expense event, even if cash does not come in or go out at that moment. For example, your utility company might send you a bill for your electricity usage, and immediately credit their invoiced amount. Placing the numbers into an automatically calculated (or formula-driven) operating projection over a period of time (we recommend a month-by-month view that spans at least three years into the future) enables easy and continuous iteration. The operating projection sheet can also be used to track any impacts that correlate with any of the financial metrics or as independent variables. For example, the sales of a certain number of products might result in biodiversity increases of a certain amount, or a certain number of employees working with the organization over a certain period of time correlates with a particular beneficial outcome. Your operating projection can be re-presented as an operating summary that shows you a year-by-year or quarter-by-quarter view. This also calculates some critical summary insights:

- How much resources (cash) would you need until you reach an operating "breakeven" (i.e., the point when the organization's operations reliably generate enough revenue to cover operating expenses)?
- When (what month or quarter of what year) is that point of breakeven?
- What impacts are you projected to achieve annually over the next few years?

Many prospective investors, including some community investors, will require an operating projection so they can assess, from their own perspective, the feasibility of the sales projection, how many people will need to be involved, the total capitalization needs (how much money) for the plan, and how the financial projection correlates with the estimated social and environmental impacts.

Since this is often requested or required, many organizations will find themselves developing (or outsourcing the development of) an operating projection that they only use for fundraising purposes. We think this is a mistake. A best practice for an operating projection is to continually update the assumptions and the forecast as new information becomes available. In effect, the projection is never done. Any time a summary is needed one can take a snapshot of the current assumptions and share it with investors or other stakeholders. Continuously updating a projection might take only 30–60 minutes a month. This would mean updating data and the forecast as well as doing a comparison between the operating projection and a monthly profit and loss statement. This comparison, or variance analysis, is critical for spotting risks, highlighting certain successes, and recalibrating goals and strategy.

No projection is ever 100 percent accurate, but you can aim for a monthly or quarterly variance of 10 percent or less. Variances of 10 percent or more are acceptable, but they indicate that something unexpected happened (e.g., more sales than expected or a sudden unplanned expense). Transparently sharing results to the entire team can improve autonomous problem solving and a sense of belonging and togetherness.

What about profit? Your operating projection can show, based on your assumptions, what amount of profit you might generate. The purpose of Next Economy organizations is not to maximize profit. An organization like World Centric (one of the case studies earlier in the book) might generate profit to retain as a cash reserve for growing their organization, but the metric that they organize around is their impact giving (corporate philanthropy) which is equal to 25 percent of their annual profits. Most Next Economy organizations aim for a minimal amount of profit for the purpose of sustaining or gradually growing their organization to enhance their beneficial impact. This can make some Next Economy company financial projections look like those of nonprofits, even if they are not incorporated as tax-exempt charitable organizations.

Open Book Management (OBM)

As mentioned in "Part 6: Culture," the basic idea of OBM is to share certain information with employees or worker-owners or other owners about the financial health of the organization. This could include the income statement, balance sheet, cash flow, or other data. Data that is useful for making decisions will be different for each organization. Customizing a dashboard or a simple summary of key performance indicators can, in its best expression, engage team members and distribute power. OBM requires training. The amount of training and the type of training will depend on each organization. Employees will need to understand what the numbers mean and how to manipulate certain numbers in order to consider scenarios such as increasing pricing, purchasing a piece of equipment, or hiring a new team member. For example, Zingerman's in Ann Arbor, MI, is a collection of ten partially integrated small businesses, employing more than 700 people, that practice OBM. The Zingerman's family of businesses generates more than $65 million a year in revenue. Workers gather weekly for a "huddle" where numbers are shared and discussed, proposals offered, and decisions made that impact the success of delivering their goods and services. The OBM approach has been so successful that they have created a training program around their practice called ZingTrain.

Prerequisites for OBM are buy-in from leadership, financial literacy training, transparency, making sure the numbers are available in a systemized way (so it is easy to produce reports), and accountability. In our experience, one of the keys to successful implementation of OBM is to make sure that if team members are going to make more autonomous decisions, then they are also held accountable for those decisions. In an OBM system, if you make a decision to purchase something such as a new piece of equipment and the company goes into negative cash flow and you have to miss a payroll, you need to be accountable for it.

Policy and Procedure

It is wise to invest in the documentation of policy and procedure. Clear documentation can be essential—especially when you are ready to hire new staff and grow the team. The process of writing out (or recording a video, if appropriate) a policy or procedure can put you in a reflective space to think about the best way to do the task. This can lead to discovering efficiencies and improvements on which you can train others. You also get organizational resilience by not being overly reliant on any one individual with implicit knowledge that the organization needs to function. One useful (albeit BAU) business book that explores this topic in detail is *Work the System* by Sam Carpenter (Greenleaf Book Group Press, 2021).

Many years ago, some of us were working with a lighting contractor that focused on replacing old lighting fixtures in commercial spaces with new, energy-efficient LED fixtures. After repeated encouragement from us, the company worked with their accountant to write out some of their basic accounting procedures. Tragically, soon after the procedure was written, the accountant had a medical emergency, was hospitalized, and could not return to work for some time. Fortunately, the staff at the company was able to follow the written procedures and perform critical functions such as issuing payroll to keep the 25-person company functioning while their accountant recovered.

Efficiency in Documentation

For teams with capacity constraints, it can be beneficial to do training and procedure documentation at the same time. The experienced team member teaches the trainee how to do the task and the trainee writes the procedure. The trainer then reviews and edits as needed. The trainee becomes the trainer to pass it on to the next staff member. In this manner you are using the growth needs of the company to determine which procedures to document first.

Aim for Continuous Improvement

Continuous improvement of systems can happen throughout the organization. Systems more than a couple of years old probably need a refresh. Team members that are responsible for the operational systems can respond to reports of challenges, errors, and bottlenecks in the organization, while also looking forward to future needs and proactively building capacity. Regardless of the stage of development, you want to know what the current priorities are while also preparing for your future needs.

Dedicate the Time and Energy

Though it can feel overwhelming, particularly for a small team, it is important to dedicate time to work on policy and procedure. Survey the organization for successes and failures. Document the procedures for the successes. Problem-solve the failures and develop new procedures. In this way you build on your strengths, and your challenges and failures become your opportunities for growth. Keep a transparent log of organization failures and learnings. For a small team, this could be a monthly, seasonal, or annual endeavor based on your ability to dedicate the necessary time and energy.

Personal Productivity

We share this section with some caution because BAU culture has an unhealthy addiction to productivity. Productivity as an end in itself can perpetuate harm and exploitation of others. At the same time, a certain focus on efficiency and effectiveness can make the difference for an organization to successfully navigate the price parity paradox. In our experience, we have found that productivity can improve by focusing on several key areas: org structure, time, tasks, and communication.

Organizational Structure

As we discussed earlier in this chapter, clarity on the overall organizational structure, decision-making authority, and assigning individual roles can help empower your team. Focusing exclusively on individual productivity—without a coherent system and clear accountabilities—will produce limited results. An effective org structure will help you to better sense tensions, blockages, and other problems as they arise. This will allow you to shift priorities and workload across the team in order to maintain overall productivity.

Time

One best practice for time management is to sketch out work blocks for your week before your week starts. For example, you may have a number of tasks to complete that require different types of attention and focus. You might have strategic planning work that requires deep concentration. You may have to respond to several customers to answer their questions about your product. You may also have to lift and organize boxes in order to restock inventory in your warehouse. Try to organize your time—from weekly to daily to hourly work blocks—to maximize your mental and physical energy levels. Inevitably, the plans you make will be disrupted or need to be modified. However, you will become more skillful over time at planning for what you can accomplish.

Set boundaries and control distractions to protect your attention. Turn off text, phone, and email notifications to maintain your focus. Coordinate with your team to let them know when you will have these uninterrupted work blocks. Let them know you will be able to respond to communications once they are over. At LIFT, our team currently has "no meeting Wednesdays" so we can accomplish more in focused work blocks. We have also seen teams that have set times (like 10 a.m. to 12 p.m.) for no meetings and no messaging so people can be more productive.

Once you have a practice of work planning, it can also be helpful to track your time to review how your time was spent compared to how you planned to use it. This insight can help you adapt your time blocks and work plan. This can be done independently or with the support of a teammate or manager.

Tasks

We recommend catching all the tasks that fall in your responsibility and categorizing them by org area or by project. This builds upon the concept presented in the previous section. The tasks you collect for a specific area will already have an associated designated work block.

Do not forget to delegate tasks to other team members as needed—especially if you need support or more capacity. Let others push back if they cannot do a task. Some training may be required in order to delegate certain items. However, the upfront time and energy you spend on training will often be regained (and more) over the long term.

Once you have caught all the tasks relevant to your role and delegated what you can, you can prioritize your remaining tasks. Most people naturally prioritize urgent and important tasks. However, depending on your role and responsibilities, you may need to balance your work plan with important and nonurgent tasks as well. These are things like strategic planning, visioning, and culture building (i.e., many of the things in the Design level of the org chart). A strategic plan, for example, may not be urgent, but it could be extremely important for the future of the organization. If you do not make consistent progress on it, you may be doing yourself and the team a disservice by deprioritizing it due to other, more urgent demands.

Another best practice is to break larger projects down into smaller, bite-sized tasks. A project that may take months to complete can be broken down into individual tasks that may take a few hours to complete. You could then fit these into your weekly or daily work plan. If you are interested in going deeper, one classic book on productivity is *Getting Things Done* by David Allen (Penguin Publishing Group, 2015).

Communication

We now have technology and communication tools that can instantaneously connect people around the globe. These tools have upsides, but they have also created a powerful and overwhelming flood of information. There is often more inbound information and messaging than one person can read and respond to. This can result in time wasted with irrelevant or unimportant information. It can also create the risk of missing critical messages or information. You can easily lose your productivity if you do not have clear, effective strategies to manage your communication flows.

The other risk, especially with text-based communications, is that they are useful for communicating and coordinating logistics, project work, details, and so on, but completely omit important information such as social cues communicated by body language and tone of voice. You must choose the appropriate time and channel for each message. For any sensitive communications (or messages that have the possibility of emotional content or reaction), in-person communication is best, then video, then audio or phone (though the body language will be missing). This awareness has profound productivity implications because getting stuck in conflict can be draining, both mentally and emotionally.

Another best practice often associated with email (but that also applies to any other messaging platform) is to keep your inbox at or near zero. For example, try to see all your messages without scrolling. Use filters to direct newsletters, group listservs, or order delivery updates to folders that can be checked later. This requires regular maintenance. When you have time to tend to your messages, first scan for messages that should not make it to your inbox (filter them out, unsubscribe, mark as spam, archive, etc.). You want to take a moment to prevent that sender or message type from distracting you again in the future. Skim through your relevant messages and clear what you can in a couple of minutes or less. Fit the longer messages (or ones that are associated with projects or tasks) into your work blocks. Note that the order of messages in your inbox is never going to line up exactly with your actual priorities. If you treat it as such, you will be choosing to subvert your actual priority for the random order of messages that you have received. Instead, bookmark them for review later. Respond to the email when that task is up for you—not when someone sent it to you. This may be uncomfortable and take some getting used to. After practicing for some time, you may realize a new level of focus and efficacy that was previously unavailable to you.

Case Study: New Frameworks Cooperative

NEWFRAMEWORKS.COM

New Frameworks is a "multi-racial, women-, queer-, and trans-owned worker cooperative committed to a kinder sort of building." They use ecologically minded building practices such as natural-material wall panel systems, timber framing, natural finishes, and reclaimed materials. New Frameworks practices high-performance natural building that supports climate justice in northern Vermont. In addition to offering worker-ownership to staff, they partner with local organizations to promote migrant justice, focusing on better labor standards and housing.

We are featuring them as a case study here because they have an interesting and innovative organizational structure. In contrast to a more traditional organizational structure, New Frameworks uses an abstract, biomimetic drawing of a plant body and rhizomal nodes to map their organizational areas. This very creative representation fits with and reinforces the innovative and organic vision and culture of the organization. It also shows there is no one right way to map an organizational structure.

NEXT ECONOMY PRINCIPLES REPRESENTED:

- 1 Meet Basic Needs
- 2 Share Ownership
- 3 Democratize Governance
- 4 Support Local Communities
- 8 Regenerate Systems
- 9 Develop People
- 10 Build Movements

9

Next Steps for
the Next Economy

Y ou have learned the key components of creating sustained impact as an organization. How do you move beyond one organization? How do you change the whole system? Successful Next Economy organizations are needed to federate and collaborate on changing things like governance systems, healthcare, education, media, and housing. The long arc of transition aims to compassionately hospice out the BAU economy and midwife in the Next Economy.

Even if there were hundreds of thousands of organizations, each expressing Next Economy principles and beneficially impacting their community and environment, that would alone be inadequate to the task of transforming the whole economic system. A broader movement is needed. This movement—similar to how chambers of commerce influence local, regional, and national government regulations to advance BAU interests—will need to coordinate many Next Economy enterprises of all sizes to influence existing government structures through lobbying and advocacy. Additionally, the public at large must organize and exercise the power of boycott and peaceful direct action in protest of the BAU economy (while simultaneously acting in alignment and in coordination with the Next Economy organizations). For the movement to be successful, it needs to be decentralized yet coordinated, inclusive, aligned in values, and, ultimately, global—similar to the antiestablishment countercultural phenomenon that developed in the 1960s. There are signs that this movement is emerging. There are a number of hubs and groups organizing to advance the conditions necessary for transformation. These include Movement Generation, The Movement for Black Lives (M4BL), American Sustainable Business Network (ASBN), The Center for Economic Democracy, Common Future, New Economy Coalition, The Rising Majority, Wellbeing Economy Alliance, Grassroots Global Justice Alliance, NDN Collective, Post Growth Institute, The Democracy Collaborative, Zebras Unite, and the U.S. Federation of Worker Cooperatives.

Case Study: The Next System Project

THENEXTSYSTEM.ORG

The Next System Project is an initiative of The Democracy Collaborative. It is aimed at bold thinking and action to address the systemic challenges—such as economic inequality, racial injustice, and climate change—the United States faces now and in coming decades. The organization uses research, strategic thinking, and on-the-ground organizing to promote visions, models, and pathways that point to a "next system" that will differ radically and in fundamental ways from the failed systems of the past and present. The next system will be capable of delivering superior social, economic, and ecological outcomes.

NEXT ECONOMY PRINCIPLES REPRESENTED:

- 2 Share Ownership
- 5 Integrate Education
- 10 Build Movements

Breakthrough Opportunities

There are a lot of things that need to change about the economy. However, we believe there are particular "gaps" (or underdeveloped areas) which, if addressed, offer the potential for large positive break-throughs. Indeed, part of the reason we wrote this book is to enroll and engage a wider audience in the work of developing these breakthrough areas. Here are some of the gaps that need the attention and discipline of values-aligned entrepreneurs:

- Distributed governance, whether that is citizen assemblies, participatory budgeting, or other models of direct democracy
- Media platforms that are consumer-owned and member-driven
- Self-directed savings and investment plans that are community-serving
- Financial systems for true-cost accounting and open-book management
- Land and housing models owned by the commons (i.e., owned by the public)
- Landback (i.e., putting Indigenous lands back in Indigenous hands) and reparations strategies
- Supply chain development and shared purchasing for the 1,000-plus worker-owned cooperatives that exist today in the United States
- Village-building and community development
- Different ways of transacting, including new and alternative currencies
- Data privacy innovations
- Open, free, and neutral common telecommunications and internet networks
- Cooperative climate insurance
- Structures and systems for incentivizing ecosystem restoration and repair work
- Reimaging retirement in communitarian (as opposed to individualistic) ways
- Accessible, free, holistic childcare for anyone who requires it

One hope we have with this book is to plant seeds about these gaps within you. Perhaps one day, when the opportunity arises to work on them, you will heed the call and find community support to help you build solutions in these sectors. The following sections go deeper into four areas where we see communities of practice already emerging.

Next Health

Our current healthcare system is tearing apart at the seams. The for-profit nature of healthcare, particularly in the United States, creates gross health inequities. Structural racism determines health outcomes. Massive profit-taking and exploitation occur at every step. The U.S. healthcare system prioritizes pharma first, in a disease triage care model that perpetuates excessive specialization, rather than looking at the human as an integral organism. Society is stuck in a system characterized by distorted costs of birth care, death, and medicine. Diet, activity, and environment are largely ignored, and mental health is marginalized. Some argue that chronic disease is on track to bankrupt the U.S. economy.

When we envision "Next Health," or the next healthcare system (that works effectively), we envision the following:

- Health is a human right.
- There is universal access to reliable care, treatment, and therapy.
- Care, in a system that treats the whole person, prevents disease and optimizes wellbeing.
- Resilience of the system is built upon education and health advocacy.
- Environmental and social determinants of health are factored into the system (e.g., housing security, racial justice, reparations, clean water, food, air, etc.).
- Consumers are empowered as agents of their own health.
- The healthcare system is owned by everyone. The profits are distributed to address the root causes that challenge the ability to provide health for all.
- Mental health first responders are sent to address emergency calls.
- A network of cooperatively owned healthcare providers actively fosters and encourages preventative wellness care. Because

the cooperatives are part of the community, the profits would go toward addressing the social determinants of health (e.g., access to affordable, safe, nontoxic homes; affordable and healthy produce, proteins, starches, and fats; and access to abundant green space for commuting, playing, convening, connecting, and exercise).

One opportunity we see is in the field of direct primary care (DPC). The DPC approach is a practice and payment model where patients/consumers pay their physician or practice directly in the form of periodic payments for a defined set of primary care services. DPC practices typically charge patients (rather than billing insurance) a flat monthly or annual fee in exchange for access to a broad range of primary care and medical administrative services. The incentives for DPC practices are to keep their patients healthy. For example, if a DPC clinic has 500 members, it cannot operate if all 500 members use the service every week. The clinic is incentivized to keep patients in optimal health so that they do not need to continually come back (since the clinic is still earning a flat fee from each member regardless of whether the service is used).

One downside of DPC groups today is that—even with its improvements on the traditional "sick-care" model of medicine—there exists an incentive to provide minimal service to as many members as possible. In the previous example, if a DPC practice had 1,000 members instead of 500 (with the same number of doctors and operational costs), the practice would be more profitable. A DPC clinic organized as a multistakeholder cooperative (owned by both the doctors and patients) could help address this incentive. For example, if the DPC practice generated profits above a certain level (meaning that more and more people were getting healthy), the patients would share the benefits—perhaps in the form of getting their membership fees back or even receiving excess profits. Alternatively, the DPC cooperative might decide to invest its profits in providing housing to some of the patients in the group that do not have access to affordable housing. Since access to stable housing is critical for optimal health, providing housing to clinic members would potentially increase the profits of the DPC cooperative in future years (as fewer sick members would mean less cost to operate). In this way, a multi-stakeholder DPC cooperative could start to address some of the social determinants of health that are usually outside the normal scope of medical care.

Does a multi-stakeholder DPC cooperative exist yet? Unfortunately no (at least we have not come across any in our years of research on this topic). There are pieces of this vision already happening in different communities. For example, innovative regional systems include Nuka System of Care in Alaska and the Ithaca Free Clinic/Ithaca Health Alliance in New York.

Anna O'Malley, director of the Natura Institute for Ecology and Medicine at Commonweal, has a practice called Community Medicine Circles. In this model, instead of seeing one patient at a time, Anna creates peer groups (of roughly 10 people) who see her all at once. Anna facilitates conversations to have members support each other to meet their individual and collective health goals. This costs a fraction of each member having an individual doctor consultation.

We are continuing to track the emergence of these and other developments in the field of Next Health. Innovations in this area are happening quickly that promise a new model of care that ensures access to health for all.

Next Education

Rethinking how the education system is designed is imperative. The principles of Next Economy enterprises can be applied to envision an education system that works for the benefit of all life. In particular, we envision a system that is

- Democratic, cooperative, and community-owned
- Self-directed, project-based, and fosters engaged human beings
- Focused on development of the whole person
- Employing multiple learning modalities
- Multicultural, multi-lingual, and embraces a multitude of perspectives

- Focused on nature-based education (childhood exposure to nature conveys many health and wellness benefits)
- Continuous and does not stop once you leave formal "school"—making learning a lifelong journey is a key part of Next Education

There are innovators who are creating, developing, and stewarding educational institutions that already include aspects (but not all) of this vision. Some of the movements we are watching in the education sector:

- Child-centered education (e.g., Boggs School, Montessori, neo-humanism, new learning culture) focuses on emotional health and experiential learning in a "state of flow," which is the deep, fulfilled focus that naturally occurs during play, self-chosen activities, and movement. The intention is to create inspiring, hands-on learning environments where learners acquire academic, creative, intellectual, emotional, and social skills playfully and at their own pace.
- Skill sharing can happen in a formal setting like a classroom, but skill sharing can also occur casually at meetups, community centers, and in people's homes. YING and Simbi are skill sharing platforms that facilitate connection to a wide range of people looking to share.
- "Unschooling" is a style of home education that allows the student's interests and curiosities to drive the path of learning. Rather than using a defined curriculum, unschoolers trust children to gain knowledge organically.
- Permaculture schools teach about permaculture—a design approach to regenerating ecosystems, creating just and peaceful communities, and thereby increasing permanence in human culture. Permaculturists, with an ethical framework and the principles of the natural world as guides, ecologically produce food, create shelter, store water, design economic and governance systems, and meet human needs through ecological design.

- Free Schools (e.g., Summerhill School in England) were created by parents, teachers, and students in opposition to contemporaneous schooling practices. They were usually small and grassroots, lacked central organization, and taught alternative curricula.
- Sudbury Schools give students complete responsibility for their own education, and the school is run by a direct democracy in which students and staff are equal citizens.
- Green School International focuses on a "living" curriculum (outdoors, in a natural environment) that educates for sustainability through community-integrated, entrepreneurial learning.

For those of you who want to go deeper into these and other topics, we recommend Zak Stein's book *Education in a Time Between Worlds: Essays on the Future of Schools, Technology, and Society* (Bright Alliance, 2019).

Next Media

Transforming the nature of the economy will likely require transforming the nature of the media system. It seems obvious that the current system of predominantly corporate-owned media outlets (underpinned by an advertising-based revenue model) is problematic. The content presented online, on television and radio, and in print is overwhelmingly geared towards sensational stories designed to draw in the consumer. Anything that generates an emotional response is given priority. Polarized conflicts are presented in a false binary. Divisive content is promoted and rewarded. The media consumer has a hard time making sense of (what appears to be) an increasingly strange and conflicted world.

What would a Next Media system look like? We have identified the following principles, through discussions, trainings, and feedback sessions:

- News journalism that is not beholden to corporate, state, or limited interests (e.g., large donors)
- In-depth stories and reporting that accommodates and embraces nuance

- Diverse reporters and journalists representing the multitude of perspectives in society
- Owned by the journalists and the readers, listeners, and viewers
- Democratic processes to determine what gets reported on and who does the reporting

Part of what is next for the Next Economy are continued experiments in multi-stakeholder media organizations that can help communities make sense of the world and their place in it. These cooperatives might be structured to generate profit, but any profit would be distributed to the producers and/or the consumers of the content. Such media institutions might have voting mechanisms to democratically determine what gets reported on, utilize citizen journalism, be more participatory and bidirectional in the flow of information, and emphasize nuanced content that serves beneficial public outcomes. Some experiments or attempts to create Next Economy media organizations, with elements that express at least some of these principles, have begun or are early in development in different parts of the world. These are a few examples:

- *The Media Co-op* (mediacoop.ca), a media organization with a cooperative structure, has been publishing grassroots journalism online in Canada since 2006. The Media Co-op is reader-funded, member-run, and written from a grassroots perspective. For the organization, "grassroots" means that when they cover a topic, they start from the people directly affected by the policies or activities in question first. They believe that once a journalist thoroughly understands the story of those directly affected, they bring their questions to those making the decisions: politicians, corporate executives, and so on. This approach stems from The Media Co-op's belief in common sense: if they start by talking to the people who have a vested interest and experience in spinning, framing, or outright lying to their own advantage, then they are not likely to get the real story. This approach also takes the position that what is happening on the ground is more important than what people with power say about what is going on.

- *Republik* (republik.ch), a German-language magazine based in Zürich, Switzerland, bills itself as a "digital magazine for politics, business, society, and culture." Funded by its readers, it espouses a rebellion against the media corporations. *Republik* is a cooperative, ad-free, and transparent. They disclose their finances, ownership, working methods, mistakes, and wages—because they are convinced that it is important to show the conditions under which journalism is produced.

- *New Internationalist* magazine (newint.org) offers analysis and global coverage of urgent issues. From conflict and migration to climate change and democracy, they attempt to place headline stories in their proper political, social, and economic context. *New Internationalist* prides themselves in covering stories that the mainstream media often ignores, instead highlighting voices from the Global South. *New Internationalist* is an independent cooperative—with no corporate advertisers—that is co-owned by their staff team and over 4,600 reader-owners.

- *Bloc By Block News* (blocbyblocknews.com), focused on Baltimore, Maryland, "envisions a world in which people from all backgrounds are not only informed, but actively engaged in political and social movements—from their blocks to their city centers and beyond." They are a media cooperative, owned by "a collective of people who have a shared interest in receiving and creating news that impacts their daily lives."

- Means TV (means.tv) is "the world's first worker-owned, post-capitalist streaming service. Means TV has a library of films, documentaries, and shows with new programming being added all the time." They have no advertisements, product placements, corporate backers, or venture capital investors. They are entirely funded by subscribers. Means TV is "building a long-standing, worker-owned media infrastructure that reflects and empowers the 99%."

Next Housing

One of the core problematic aspects of the BAU economy is the imposed pattern of housing common to the affluent world. This pattern is problematic for a number of reasons:

- Homes (attached to the land they sit on) are owned as speculative, market assets, designed for single families with too much underutilized space.
- Housing is segregated from the other functions of life, requiring cars and other forms of transportation.
- Most homes are inappropriately oriented to the sun. This requires enormous heating and cooling energy expenditures and cost.
- Homes are made of sometimes toxic materials that are transported great distances.
- Structures are often assembled by exploited labor.
- Homes are sited and built to be vulnerable to fire, flood, and other extreme weather events.
- Housing is often situated in landscapes that are not designed to work with the environment.

Many organizations are working on the means of resolving each aspect of this larger pattern. Few organizations are working on systemically transforming the nature of how society thinks about housing for an increasingly unstable climate future.

The major shift in principles will be to think of access to healthy, permanently affordable housing as a universal human right. This will likely require reconsidering land from being "owned" by individuals and corporations to being "stewarded" in common by communities. Community land trusts, permanent real estate cooperatives, and other community-controlled, community-owned, limited equity land stewardship strategies are being experimented with and developed. The intent of many of these models is to ensure long-term affordability, forestall displacement, return land rights back to original inhabitants, create wealth in low-income and BIPOC communities, and remove housing from the speculative real estate market. They are small and early in development but are gaining traction and building on what is working.

Another area of Next Economy innovation is the forms of housing, neighborhood developments, and integration into the landscape and place. Various models of cohousing (intentional, semi-communal housing—typically consisting of a cluster of private homes and a shared community space) are being trialed. Smaller and combined living spaces (tiny homes and multifamily, midsized, two- to four-story or "missing middle" housing forms) are being popularized and developed to use less material, reduce operational resource use, and increase interaction. Mixed-use design of walkable neighborhoods and innovations in zoning to accommodate small, integrated settlements is also being tested. However, these are still not "normal" and not often integrated with commons stewardship models. These are some features of Next Economy housing models:

- Passive solar design that takes advantage of a building's site, climate, and materials to minimize energy use. A well-designed passive solar home first reduces heating and cooling loads through energy-efficiency strategies and then meets those reduced loads in whole or part with solar energy.

- Biotecture that integrates plants into walls and roofs for cooling, insulation, stormwater retention, and biodiversity.

- Edible landscaping that includes plants whose fruits, foliage, flowers, roots, or other parts can be eaten.

- Conservation hydrology features. Conservation hydrology utilizes the disciplines of ecology, biology, geography, economics, anthropology, philosophy, planning, and history to guide community-based watershed literacy, planning, and action. It advocates that human development decisions must move toward rehydration of the land (when it rains, try to slow the water down, spread the water out, and sink it into the land).

- Greywater systems that use water from your bathroom sinks, showers, tubs, and washing machines. The easiest way to use greywater is to pipe it directly outside and use it to water ornamental plants or fruit trees.

- Compost toilets, which use natural processes to turn human waste into a valuable soil amendment.

- Solar photovoltaics (also called solar cells) that convert sunlight directly into electricity. Solar water heating is heating water by sunlight.

- Tightly insulated building envelopes to enable homes to produce more energy than they use.

- Food growing right outside the kitchen door to reduce the enormous challenge of food waste.

These are all being developed—but mostly in siloed efforts. Even the materials that homes are made of are undergoing Next Economy transformations. Organizations are working with fire-resistant, earthen materials and covers such as cob, straw bale, rammed earth, timber frame, cross laminated timber, and other hybrid materials. These can be sourced locally to create buildings that can be designed for resilience and operational efficiency.

Most of the existing projects today are small experiments. Few are cooperative or structured in ways that intend any surpluses generated to serve the workers or community. Little coordination exists among these efforts, even though each of these areas is related to housing humans. We are expecting to see more cooperative real estate development organizations emerge that combine elements of a transformative model of Next Economy housing. We also anticipate seeing novel forms of community cooperative insurance and a plethora of community ownership models become more popular.

Case Study: Homeless Garden Project

HOMELESSGARDENPROJECT.ORG

Compared to other counties of similar size in the United States in 2014, the unhoused population in Santa Cruz County, California, ranked among the top four, with 3,529 houseless individuals. Operating an organic farm and related enterprises including a workshop and retail and online stores, the Homeless Garden

(continued)

Project (HGP), a Santa Cruz–based nonprofit, provides job training, transitional employment, and support services to people who are houseless. HGP's transitional jobs program provides real work experience and income, as well as a supportive community environment that connects trainees to the services needed to succeed. The program makes it possible for people who are unhoused and unemployed to obtain stable housing and secure employment. By engaging the entire Santa Cruz County community in this effort, HGP addresses the root causes of houselessness, supports destigmatizing, and builds self-sufficiency for unhoused individuals. HGP's 12-month program is incredibly successful with 92 percent of its graduates obtaining jobs and housing because of the program. Since its founding, more than 600 people have participated in the project's paid job-training program.

NEXT ECONOMY PRINCIPLES REPRESENTED:

- 1 Meet Basic Needs
- 2 Share Ownership
- 4 Support Local Communities
- 6 Promote Open Source
- 8 Regenerate Systems
- 9 Develop People

Next Economy Roles

It can be overwhelming to consider your next actions. There is so much to do and so much unmet need. The work to be done is often hard. There may be little or no public recognition of your effort. Your work may be unpaid, high risk, and low reward. Certain aspects of this work are not for everyone. Your context (i.e., your privilege and positionality) influences what you might be able to take on (or not) in manifesting these possibilities. Therefore, it can be helpful to remember that the work of transitioning to the Next Economy requires many roles. If you are an entrepreneur or intrapreneur, this book has hopefully given you lots of ideas to grow the Next Economy. Here are some ideas for other roles you could play:

- *Idea dreamers:* Being an ideas person is valuable. Dreaming of a possibility and sharing it with a friend, neighbor, local politician, funder, or others can be helpful along the journey.

- *Scaffolders:* Many new initiatives are already underway. Finding them and becoming part of them—providing structure, support, and scaffolding—can help those ideas flourish. Helping existing initiatives innovate can be more secure than starting something new.

- *Starters:* Become a creator. Starting a new endeavor in an area with entrenched BAU interests can be difficult. Financial remuneration may be limited, but the rewards and potential beneficial impact can be significant. In many areas, founders or creators who understand the technical and/or arcane components of different systems (e.g., lawyers, nurses, bankers) can be particularly effective at helping things shift.

- *Supporters, advocates, and investors:* Being an advocate, supporter, customer, or a champion for new and existing efforts is incredibly valuable.

- *Researchers and learners:* The way humans live on this planet needs to be reimagined. Society desperately needs the courage and creativity of folks who love to learn about (and share) new models of operating, collaborating, and connecting.

What's Next for You in the Next Economy?

Thank you for your interest in and commitment to creating a bioregional, locally self-reliant, and racially just economy that works for the benefit of all life—one that meets the basic needs for all people everywhere while regenerating planetary ecosystems. We would like to stay in relationship with you.

If you would like to go deeper into the topics discussed in this book, please consider joining one of the facilitated Next Economy MBA online courses. New cohorts are offered every spring and summer. You can also download the free *Next Economy MBA: Read-Along Workbook* at lifteconomy.com/mbabook to go deeper into the content of this book. Other opportunities to stay engaged include signing up for our monthly newsletter, subscribing to our *Next Economy Now* podcast, attending one of our self-study training sessions, participating in one of our upcoming Next Economy online summits, or dropping us a line to tell us what you are working on. We want to learn from you and be helpful to you if we can. If you have a highlight to share or critique to offer, please send us your feedback. We also encourage you to support any of the organizations profiled in this book (financially, by volunteering, lifting up and promoting, and more). Your participation in a collective vision for the Next Economy is essential.

As we have mentioned in the introduction, we joyfully acknowledge that there are whispers, songs, dances, and actions that point to the radical transformation that is already underway all around us. This feeling is eloquently expressed by James Baldwin:

> *An old world is dying and a new one, kicking in the belly of its mother, time, announces that it is ready to be born. This birth will not be easy, and many of us are doomed to discover that we are exceedingly clumsy midwives. No matter, so long as we accept that our responsibility is to the newborn: the acceptance of responsibility contains the key to the necessarily evolving skill.*
>
> —*James Baldwin*, No Name in the Street (*credit to Miliaku Nwabueze of MBA Cohort III for bringing this quote to our attention*)

Thank you for helping us hospice out the old economy and midwife in the new. We are honored to be a part of this journey with you. To stay in touch with us, please email us at contact@lifteconomy.com or visit lifteconomy.com/mbabook for access to free resources.

NOTES

1. LaDuke, Winona, "Doula to the New Economy," Minnesota Women's Press (blog), June 1, 2019. https://www.womenspress.com/being-a-doula-to-the-next-economy/.

2. "From Banks and Tanks to Caring and Cooperation: A Strategic Framework for a Just Transition," Movement Generation, accessed October 18, 2022. https://movementgeneration.org/wp-content/uploads/2016/11/JT_booklet_Eng_printspreads.pdf.

3. "Ten Richest Men Double Their Fortunes in Pandemic While Incomes of 99 Percent of Humanity Fall," Oxfam International, January 17, 2022. https://www.oxfam.org/en/press-releases/ten-richest-men-double-their-fortunes-pandemic-while-incomes-99-percent-humanity.

4. Majendie, Adam, "Without Clearing Any Farmland, We Could Feed Two Earths' Worth of People," Bloomberg.com, December 14, 2020. https://www.bloomberg.com/news/features/2020-12-15/no-more-hunger-how-to-feed-everyone-on-earth-with-just-the-land-we-have.

5. "Progress on Household Drinking Water, Sanitation and Hygiene 2000–2020: Five Years into the SDGs," WHO/UNICEF Joint Monitoring Programme, accessed October 18, 2022. https://washdata.org/sites/default/files/2021-07/jmp-2021-wash-households.pdf.

6. Leahy, Stephen, "One Million Species at Risk of Extinction, UN Report Warns," National Geographic, accessed May 3, 2021. https://www.nationalgeographic.com/environment/article/ipbes-un-biodiversity-report-warns-one-million-species-at-risk.

7. "Climate Change: A Threat to Human Wellbeing and Health of the Planet. Taking Action Now Can Secure Our Future," IPCC, accessed October 17, 2022. https://www.ipcc.ch/2022/02/28/pr-wgii-ar6/.

8. Byman, Daniel L., The Brookings Institution, Spreading Hate: The Global Rise of White Supremacist Terrorism, Oxford University Press, March 22, 2022. https://www.brookings.edu/books/spreading-hate-the-global-rise-of-white-supremacist-terrorism/.

9. Saraiva, Catarina, "Black-White Wealth Gap Getting Worse, 160 Years of US Data Show," Bloomberg.com, June 7, 2022. https://www.bloomberg.com/news/articles/2022-06-07/black-white-wealth-gap-getting-worse-160-years-of-us-data-show.

10. Ravani, Sarah, "Oakland Saw a 24% Surge in Its Homeless Population despite Efforts to Tackle the Crisis," San Francisco Chronicle, May 16, 2022. https://www.sfchronicle.com/eastbay/article/Oakland-saw-a-24-surge-in-its-homeless-17176429.php.

11. Ho, Vivian, "Mothers Who Occupied Vacant Oakland House Will Be Allowed to Buy It," The Guardian, January 20, 2020. https://www.theguardian.com/us-news/2020/jan/21/mothers-who-occupied-vacant-oakland-house-will-be-allowed-to-buy-it.

12. Kubiszewski, Ida, Robert Costanza, Carol Franco, Philip Lawn, John Talberth, Tim Jackson, and Camille Aylmer, "Beyond GDP: Measuring and Achieving Global Genuine Progress," Ecological Economics 93 (September 2013): 57–68. https://doi.org/10.1016/j.ecolecon.2013.04.019.

13. "World Game," Buckminster Fuller Institute, accessed February 11, 2022. https://www.bfi.org/about-fuller/big-ideas/world-game/.

14. Cahn, Edgar S., No More Throw-Away People: The Co-Production Imperative (Washington, D.C.: Essential Books, 2004), 61.

15. Laloux, Frederic, Reinventing Organizations: A Guide to Creating Organizations Inspired by the Next Stage in Human Consciousness (self-published, 2014; https://www.reinventingorganizations.com/).

16. Mitchell, Stacy, "Key Studies: Why Independent Matters," Institute for Local Self-Reliance, accessed November 17, 2020. https://ilsr.org/key-studies-why-local-matters/.

17. "The Local Multiplier Effect," American Independent Business Alliance, accessed May 30, 2022. https://amiba.net/project/local-multiplier-effect/.

18. Institute for Local Self-Reliance, "Share of Deposits by Size of Institution, 1994 to 2018," May 14, 2019. https://ilsr.org/distribution-of-deposits-by-size-of-financial-institution/.

19. Institute for Local Self-Reliance, "Small Business Lending by Size of Institution, 2018." Institute for Local Self-Reliance, May 14, 2019. https://ilsr.org/small-business-lending-by-size-of-institution-2014/.

20. Amer, Yasmin, "In the Berkshires, a Bold Experiment with Local Currency Goes Digital," WBUR news, July 7, 2022. https://www.wbur.org/news/2022/07/07/berkshares-local-currency-crypto-digital.

21. Bollier, David and Helfrich, Silke, eds., Patterns of Commoning (Common Strategies Group in cooperation with Off the Common Books, January 1, 2015). https://patternsofcommoning.org/we-are-one-big-conversation-commoning-in-venezuela/.

22. Kahn, Karen, "Evergreen Cooperatives Adapt and Grow," Fifty by Fifty, March 31, 2021. https://www.fiftybyfifty.org/2021/03/evergreen-cooperatives-adapt-and-grow/.

23. Kegan, Robert, Lisa Lahey, Andy Fleming, and Matthew Miller, "Making Business Personal," Harvard Business Review 1404 (April 2014). https://hbr.org/2014/04/making-business-personal.

24. "Mission, Vision, Values," Center for Racial Justice in Education, accessed October 17, 2022. https://centerracialjustice.org/mission-vision-values/.

25. Fernandes, Jason and Janelle Orsi, "Rethinking Retirement Savings," 134 Harvard Law Review L. Rev. F. 348 (April 20, 2021). https://ssrn.com/abstract=3830803.

26. Ludwig, Ma'ikwe, "Comparing Cultural Worldviews," Together Resilient: Building Community in the Age of Climate Disruption (Rutledge, MO: Fellowship for Intentional Community, 2017), 134.

27. Goebel, Bryan, "How the Internet Archive Provides Below-Market Housing to Employees," KQED, April 7, 2015. https://www.kqed.org/news/10481408/how-the-internet-archive-provides-below-market-housing-to-employees.

28. de Morree, Pim, "Self-Set Salaries: A Practical Guide," Corporate Rebels, October 2, 2022. https://corporate-rebels.com/self-set-salaries/.

29. "Partners for a Hunger Free Oregon: Equitable Merit Compensation Policy," Harmonize, accessed October 18, 2022. https://harmonize.work/wp-content/uploads/Harmonize_PHFOCompensationPolicy.pdf.

30. Lorde, Audre, "Age, Race, Class and Sex: Women Redefining Difference," Paper delivered at the Copeland Colloquium, Amherst College, April 1980. https://www.colorado.edu/odece/sites/default/files/attached-files/rba09-sb4converted_8.pdf.

ACKNOWLEDGMENTS

We want to express our deep gratitude to the inspiring, loving, and supportive people who helped make this book possible. In particular, we want to say thank you to

- All of our Next Economy MBA online course alumni
- Edgar Villanueva for the foreword
- Miliaku Nwabueze for analyzing our online course and helping to make it better
- Jenny Kassan, Ana Ramos, abdiel j. lópez, Steve Dubb, Mike Strode, and Rob Dietz for giving us your helpful thoughts, comments, and edits on our manuscript
- Neal Maillet and Jeevan Sivasubramaniam at Berrett-Koehler for agreeing to publish this book
- All of the Next Economy organizations featured in this book for inspiring us with your work
- And finally, to all of our families, who supported us through this process

We could not have done it without the support of each of you and this broader community. Thank you!

INDEX

Note: Information in figures is indicated by page numbers in *italics*.

ABOUT THE AUTHORS

Erin Axelrod is a partner at LIFT Economy, helping to accelerate the spread of businesses that benefit the climate, specializing in enterprises that address soil and water regeneration. She is a grassroots organizer and an amateur ecologist. Her clients have included Winona's Hemp & Heritage Farm, Jonas Philanthropies, Buckminster Fuller Institute, Native Conservancy, Sunken Seaweed, Salt Point Seaweed, Singing Frogs Farm, Daily Acts, Fibershed, North Coast Brewing Company, and MycoWorks. She is cofounder of the Force for Good Fund, the first crowdfunded accelerator and development fund supporting a more diverse, inclusive economy through social enterprise. She also convenes LIFT Economy's Regenerative Agriculture Investor's Network (RAIN) and a Restorative Ocean Economies Field-Building Initiative. She co-initiated the launch of The Next Egg, a collaborative project to support citizens to move the $32 trillion in U.S. retirement savings away from Wall Street and onto Main Street.

Erin is an expert in business design, planning, and systems development. As a facilitator, she focuses on effective process management, shared values alignment, and customized project planning.

When not working, she loves to plant trees and harvest wild foods in the forest ecosystems around her home, including mushrooms, huckleberries, elderberries, and bay nuts to make nutrient-dense foods for her community. A frequent public speaker, she has given presentations at conferences including Social Capital Markets Conference (SOCAP), Permaculture Voices, Food Funded, Sustainable Enterprise Conference, NorCal Permaculture Convergence, the Indigenous Hemp Conference, and the CA Greywater Conference.

She received her Permaculture Design Certificate with Toby Hemenway in 2011 and has worked on projects ever since to support an economy that works for the benefit of all life, with no one left out.

Kevin Bayuk's roots are in entrepreneurship and activism. After immersing himself in all aspects of starting and growing companies, Kevin focused his attention on learning about and teaching ecosystemic design. Kevin merges his experience in business with his experience in permaculture design to help organizations care for people while regenerating and repairing the earth's ecosystems. He frequently teaches classes and workshops, does public speaking, facilitates planning, and provides one-on-one mentoring as a founding partner of the Urban Permaculture Institute. Kevin also serves as the senior financial fellow at Project Drawdown, developing the business case to address climate change through existing practices and technologies. Additionally, Kevin provides impact investment strategy to the RiverStyx Foundation. Kevin has helped design and start food security gardens and public learning experiences intent on reminding people that we, too, are nature. Kevin has raised millions of dollars to capitalize business operations, led large teams, and can speak well to the benefits and pitfalls of raising capital and the many paths of growing a Next Economy organization.

Shawn Berry is an organizational strategist inspired to harness the power of business to create resilient local economies as patterns to be documented, open sourced, scaled globally, and adapted regionally. Shawn left an early career path in nuclear physics research to found the Woodshanti Cooperative (1997–2011), a custom cabinet and furniture shop in San Francisco that set the standard for ethical craftsmanship in the green building movement. This hands-on experience as an entrepreneur combined with community organizing and systems theory to craft the vision for LIFT Economy to model an economy that works for all life.

Shawn is especially gifted at assessing and addressing gaps in the ways in which businesses and lives are organized. He has remarkable skills in being able to stay present in the often chaotic environment of leading a business, as he helps clients craft and adapt frameworks and models to enable them to be more efficient and effective. Shawn's experience with working in democratic, multi-stakeholder work environments enables him to offer invaluable counseling in organizing business structures and communicating effectively with partners, employees, and board members.

Ryan Honeyman is a partner and worker-owner at LIFT Economy and co-author of *The B Corp Handbook: How to Use Business as a Force for Good* (Berrett-Koehler Publishers, 2019). Ryan has helped more than 50 companies—including Patagonia, Allbirds, Ben & Jerry's, King Arthur Flour, Tanka Bar, Animikii, and Red Bay Coffee—become Certified B Corporations, recertify as B Corporations, and maximize the value of their B Corp certification.

Ryan provides diversity, equity, and inclusion consulting services to B Corps and other social enterprises. Ryan has a particular focus on working with other white-identified folks (particularly companies that are white-led and/or majority white) to help educate, organize, and mobilize "our own" as part of a multiracial, cross-class movement towards collective liberation.

Along with his LIFT Economy team, Ryan helped cofound the Force for Good Fund, a million-dollar fund that invests in women- and people-of-color-owned, Best for the World B Corps (those that score in the top 10 percent of all B Corps worldwide). He is also a cohost of *Next Economy Now,* a LIFT podcast highlighting the leaders who are taking a regenerative, bioregional, democratic, transparent, and whole-systems approach to using business for good.

Ryan has written articles for the *Stanford Social Innovation Review, Fast Company, Entrepreneur, Huffington Post, Utne Reader,* and *TriplePundit.* He has been a featured speaker at SOCAP, Bioneers, Summit LA, the B Corp Champions Retreat, the Sustainable Enterprise Conference, the Hong Kong Social Enterprise Summit, the Stanford d.school, the Wharton School of Business, the UC Berkeley Haas School of Business, and many others.

Phoenix Soleil is a teacher of nonviolent communication and mindfulness and has a passion for developing people, teams, and organizations. She has led trainings in communication, racial justice, personal development, theater improvisation, and play for individuals, groups, and organizations such as Google, the Kellogg Foundation, Mind Body Awareness Project, and Search Inside Yourself Leadership Institute.

As a teacher and committed practitioner of the insight meditation tradition, she was nominated and selected for Spirit Rock's Community Dharma Leaders Program, and has taught at East Bay Meditation Center. Her deep practice includes several silent meditation retreats of two months or more. Phoenix is also an affiliate trainer for Race Forward: The Center for Racial Justice Innovation, where she offers organizational development training focused on increasing inclusion and diversity in the workplace.

ABOUT LIFT ECONOMY

Mission: LIFT Economy is an impact consulting firm whose mission is to create, model, and share a racially just, regenerative, and locally self-reliant economy that works for the benefit of all life.

Vision: A world that works for all. We meet human needs in ways that benefit all life. We see every person on the earth with adequate access to basic needs and opportunities and we see thriving ecosystems increasing in biodiversity and abundance.

Core Values:

- *Collective liberation:* We address historical and present harm rooted in an active underlying care and compassion for all.

- *Joy:* We express joy and wellbeing to model and inspire the journey to a liberated and just society. We take responsibility for creating joy and play in our work lives.

- *Authenticity:* We practice and commit to being honest and vulnerable in our communication as a team and with other stakeholders. We aspire to be self-reflective as individuals and as an organization.

- *Impact:* Service with discernment. We value beneficial results or outcomes. We also believe in serving others in a way that is beneficial to them and their mission but also mutually beneficial for life. Our work is an expression of a purpose that is larger than ourselves.

- Since our founding in 2011, we have helped grow the Next Economy by
  - Consulting with 300-plus mission-aligned businesses and organizations
  - Raising $1.1 million and deploying non-extractive investments to 13 women- and/or person-of-color-owned businesses via the Force for Good Fund
  - Producing more than 300 episodes of the *Next Economy Now* podcast to elevate the voices of leading entrepreneurs, activists, and authors. The podcast has received 500,000 listens as of 2023.
  - Guiding hundreds of participants in more than 10 cohorts of the Next Economy MBA online course
  - Helping more than 75 companies achieve B Corp certification. LIFT's own B Corp score places it among the top 25 highest-scoring B Corps in the world
  - Growing as a worker-owned cooperative
- Helping organize larger "field building" projects, such as
  - The Next Egg project to transform notions about retirement
  - The Regenerative Agriculture Investor Network (RAIN) to organize investors, philanthropists, and entrepreneurs committed to moving beyond "sustainable" to regenerative agriculture
  - Restorative Ocean Economies to support organizations focused on open-source methodologies for accelerating the adoption of replicable, worker-owned solutions for restoring ocean health while meeting food, fertilizer, fuel, ecosystem, and habitat needs
  - Building Resilient Communities to support the development of carbon-sequestering building by helping bring together the stakeholders and communities that are enabling these techniques to scale

There are many other initiatives that we are working on at any given moment. Check out the LIFT website at lifteconomy.com to learn more about us and our latest projects.

Dear reader,

Thank you for picking up this book and welcome to the worldwide BK community! You're joining a special group of people who have come together to create positive change in their lives, organizations, and communities.

What's BK all about?

Our mission is to connect people and ideas to create a world that works for all.

Why? Our communities, organizations, and lives get bogged down by old paradigms of self-interest, exclusion, hierarchy, and privilege. But we believe that can change. That's why we seek the leading experts on these challenges—and share their actionable ideas with you.

A welcome gift

To help you get started, we'd like to offer you a **free copy** of one of our bestselling ebooks:

www.bkconnection.com/welcome

When you claim your **free ebook**, you'll also be subscribed to our blog.

Our freshest insights

Access the best new tools and ideas for leaders at all levels on our blog at ideas.bkconnection.com.

Sincerely,

Your friends at Berrett-Koehler

Certified

Corporation